First World War
and Army of Occupation
War Diary
France, Belgium and Germany

66 DIVISION
199 Infantry Brigade
Manchester Regiment
2/8th Battalion
14 March 1917 - 13 February 1918

WO95/3145/4

The Naval & Military Press Ltd
www.nmarchive.com
Published in association with The National Archives

Published by

The Naval & Military Press Ltd

Unit 10 Ridgewood Industrial Park,

Uckfield, East Sussex,

TN22 5QE England

Tel: +44 (0) 1825 749494

www.naval-military-press.com

www.nmarchive.com

This diary has been reprinted in facsimile from the original. Any imperfections are inevitably reproduced and the quality may fall short of modern type and cartographic standards.

© **Crown Copyright**
Images reproduced by permission of The National Archives, London, England, 2015.

Contents

Document type	Place/Title	Date From	Date To
Heading	WO95/3145/4 2/8 Battalion Manchester Reg.		
Heading	199th Infy Bde 2-8th Bn Manch Regt 1915 Sep-1916 Feb 1917 Mar-1918 Feb		
War Diary	Boulogne	14/03/1917	18/03/1917
War Diary	Annequin	19/03/1917	22/03/1917
War Diary	Cambrin Left Sector	23/03/1917	27/03/1917
War Diary	Cambrin (New) Right Sector	27/03/1917	27/03/1917
War Diary	Cambrin Sector	28/03/1917	30/03/1917
War Diary	Cambrin Right	31/03/1917	31/03/1917
War Diary	War Diary of 2/8 Bn The Manchester Regt From March 4th To March 31st 1917 Volume 1		
Miscellaneous	Appendix "B"		
Operation(al) Order(s)	2/8th Battalion Manchester Regt Order No. 1	18/03/1917	18/03/1917
Operation(al) Order(s)	2/8th Batt Manchester Regiment Order No. 2	23/03/1917	23/03/1917
Operation(al) Order(s)	2/8th Battalion Manchester Regiment Order No. 3	27/03/1917	27/03/1917
Operation(al) Order(s)	2/7th Battalion Manchester Regiment Order No. 6	30/03/1917	30/03/1917
Miscellaneous	Time Table		
Miscellaneous	Appendix C		
Miscellaneous	Casualties		
Miscellaneous	Appendix B Maps		
Map	Map		
Heading	War Diary of 2/8th Bn Manchester Regiment From 1st April 1917 To 30th April 1917 Volume I		
War Diary	Cambrin Right	01/04/1917	04/04/1917
War Diary	Noyelles	05/04/1917	08/04/1917
War Diary	Cambrin Right	09/04/1917	12/04/1917
War Diary	Cambrin Sector	13/04/1917	16/04/1917
War Diary	Cambrin Right	17/04/1917	20/04/1917
War Diary	Noyelles	21/04/1917	24/04/1917
War Diary	St Elie Right	25/04/1917	30/04/1917
War Diary	Noyelles	02/05/1917	05/05/1917
War Diary	(Trenches) Cambrin Right	06/05/1917	12/05/1917
War Diary	B5 M17 Support	18/05/1917	18/05/1917
War Diary	Cambrin Right	18/05/1917	26/05/1917
War Diary	Noyelles	27/05/1917	01/06/1917
Heading	War Diary of 2/8th Bn. Manchester Regiment From 1st May 1917 To 31st May 1917 (Volume I)		
Miscellaneous	Appendix A Operation Orders		
Operation(al) Order(s)	2/8th Batt Manchester Regiment Order No. 11	05/05/1917	05/05/1917
Miscellaneous	Time And Route Table	06/05/1917	06/05/1917
Operation(al) Order(s)	2/8th Bn Manchester Regiment Order No. 12	11/05/1917	11/05/1917
Miscellaneous	Relief Table	12/05/1917	12/05/1917
Operation(al) Order(s)	2/8th Batt Manchester Regt Order No. 13	12/05/1917	12/05/1917
Miscellaneous	Relief Table	13/05/1917	18/05/1917
Operation(al) Order(s)	2/8th Batt Manchester Regiment Order No. 14	23/05/1917	23/05/1917
Operation(al) Order(s)	2/8th Bn Manchester Regt Order No. 15	25/05/1917	25/05/1917
Miscellaneous	Relief Table	27/05/1917	27/05/1917
Operation(al) Order(s)	2/8th Batt Manchester Regiment Order No. 6	01/06/1917	01/06/1917
Heading	War Diary of 2/8th Manchester Regiment From 1st June 1917 To 30th June 1917 (Volume I)		

War Diary	Noyelles "B" & "C" Coys Camrin Left	02/06/1917	02/06/1917
War Diary	Noyelles "B" & "D" Coys Cambrin Left	03/06/1917	03/06/1917
War Diary	Noyelles	04/06/1917	04/06/1917
War Diary	Cambrin Right	05/06/1917	10/06/1917
War Diary	Support	11/06/1917	17/06/1917
War Diary	Cambrin Right	17/06/1917	21/06/1917
War Diary	La. Pugnoy (Billets)	22/06/1917	25/06/1917
War Diary	St Pol	26/06/1917	02/07/1917
Miscellaneous	Appendix A Operation Orders		
Operation(al) Order(s)	2/8th Batt Manchester Regiment Order No. 16	01/06/1917	01/06/1917
Operation(al) Order(s)	2/8th Batt Manchester Regt Order No. 17	03/06/1917	03/06/1917
Operation(al) Order(s)	2/8th Batt Manchester Regt Order No. 18	03/06/1917	03/06/1917
Operation(al) Order(s)	2/8th Batt Manchester Regiment Order No. 19	03/06/1917	03/06/1917
Operation(al) Order(s)	2/8th Bn Manchester Regiment Order No. 20	04/06/1917	04/06/1917
Miscellaneous	Time & Route Table		
Operation(al) Order(s)	2/8th Bn Manchester Regt Order No. 21	10/06/1917	10/06/1917
Operation(al) Order(s)	2/8th Bn Manchester Regiment Order No. 22	16/06/1917	16/06/1917
Miscellaneous	Relief Table	17/06/1917	17/06/1917
Operation(al) Order(s)	2/8th Bn Manchester Regiment Order No. 23	21/06/1917	21/06/1917
Operation(al) Order(s)	2/8th Bn Manchester Regt Order No. 24	24/06/1917	24/06/1917
Miscellaneous	Map		
Map	Map		
Heading	War Diary of 2/8th Batt Manchester Regt. From July 1st 1917 To July 31st 1917 (Volume I)		
War Diary	St. Pol	02/07/1917	08/07/1917
War Diary	Courdekerque-Branch	09/07/1917	11/07/1917
War Diary	Ghyveldle	12/07/1917	14/07/1917
War Diary	Oost. Dunkerque Bains	15/07/1917	27/07/1917
War Diary	Coast Defence St. Idesbald	28/07/1917	29/07/1917
War Diary	Oost Dunkerque	30/07/1917	30/07/1917
War Diary	Right Sub.Sector Nieuport Bains Sector	31/07/1917	31/07/1917
Miscellaneous	Operation Orders A1 to A8		
Miscellaneous	2/8th Bn. Manchester Regt.	08/07/1917	08/07/1917
Miscellaneous	March Table	12/07/1917	12/07/1917
Miscellaneous	March Table		
Operation(al) Order(s)	2/8th Batt Manchester Regiment Operation Order No. 26	12/07/1917	12/07/1917
Operation(al) Order(s)	2/8th Batt Manchester Regiment Operation Order No. 27	15/07/1917	15/07/1917
Operation(al) Order(s)	2/8th Bn Manchester Regiment Order No. 28	20/07/1917	20/07/1917
Operation(al) Order(s)	2/8th Battalion Manchester Regiment Order No. 29	24/07/1917	24/07/1917
Operation(al) Order(s)	2/8th Batt Manchester Regiment Operation Order No. 30	27/07/1917	27/07/1917
Operation(al) Order(s)	2/8th Batt Manchester Regiment Order No. 31	30/07/1917	30/07/1917
Operation(al) Order(s)	2/8th Batt Manchester Regiment Operation Order No. 32	30/07/1917	30/07/1917
Heading	War Diary of 2/8th Batt. Manchester Regiment From August 1st 1917 To August 31st 1917 Volume 1		
War Diary	Nieuport Bains Sector (Right Sub-Sector)	01/08/1917	11/08/1917
War Diary	Camp. Yorkshire (Juniac)	12/08/1917	16/08/1917
War Diary	Camp Wiltshire	20/08/1917	31/08/1917
Miscellaneous	Appendices A (1) & A (2)		
Operation(al) Order(s)	2/8th Battalion Manchester Regiment Order No. 33	11/08/1917	11/08/1917
Operation(al) Order(s)	2/8th Batt Manchester Regiment Order No. 34	19/08/1917	19/08/1917
Heading	War Diary of 2/8th Batt. Manchester Regt. From 1st Sept-30th Sept 1917 Volume VII		

Type	Description	Start	End
War Diary	Wiltshire Camp Coxyde Bains	01/09/1917	01/09/1917
War Diary	Wiltshire Camp	02/09/1917	04/09/1917
War Diary	St Idesbald Cardiff Camp	05/09/1917	05/09/1917
War Diary	St Idesbald	06/09/1917	15/09/1917
War Diary	St Idesbald Cardiff Camp	16/09/1917	16/09/1917
War Diary	St Idesbald	17/09/1917	19/09/1917
War Diary	R.S.S Nieuport Bains	20/09/1917	24/09/1917
War Diary	St Idesbald	25/09/1917	25/09/1917
War Diary	Ghyvelde	26/09/1917	28/09/1917
War Diary	Renescure Area	29/09/1917	30/09/1917
Operation(al) Order(s)	2/8th Batt Manchester Regiment Order No. 35	02/09/1917	02/09/1917
Operation(al) Order(s)	2/8th Battalion Manchester Regiment Order No. 36	18/09/1917	18/09/1917
Operation(al) Order(s)	2/8th Batt Manchester Regt Order No. 37	24/09/1917	24/09/1917
Operation(al) Order(s)	2/8th Batt Manchester Regiment Order No. 38	25/09/1917	25/09/1917
Operation(al) Order(s)	2/8th Batt Manchester Regiment Order No. 39	26/09/1917	26/09/1917
Heading	2/8th Batt. Manchester Reg. War Diary October 1917		
War Diary	Renescure Area	01/10/1917	02/10/1917
War Diary	Brandhoek Erie Camp	03/10/1917	03/10/1917
War Diary	Brandhoek	04/10/1917	04/10/1917
War Diary	Vlamertinghe	05/10/1917	05/10/1917
War Diary	Support Sector D 16 C O Q To D 16 C Q 2 Sheet 2 8	06/10/1917	06/10/1917
War Diary	Left Front Sector D 16 C 6.3 To D16 B 4.6 Sheet 28	07/10/1917	10/10/1917
War Diary	Brandhoek	11/10/1917	13/10/1917
War Diary	Arques	14/10/1917	31/10/1917
Heading	War Diary Appendices And Casualties For October 1917		
Operation(al) Order(s)	2/8th Battalion Manchester Regiment Order No. 40	02/10/1917	02/10/1917
Miscellaneous	2/8th Battalion Manchester Regiment Refce Sheet 28 1/40,000 Order No. 41	05/10/1917	05/10/1917
Operation(al) Order(s)	2/8th Battn Manchester Regiment Order No. 42	06/10/1917	06/10/1917
Operation(al) Order(s)	2/8th Battn Manchester Regiment Order No. 43	10/10/1917	10/10/1917
Operation(al) Order(s)	2/8th Batt Manchester Regiment Operation Order No. 44	12/10/1917	12/10/1917
Miscellaneous	War Diary		
Miscellaneous	2/8th Batt. Manchester Regt		
Heading	War Diary November 1917 2/8 Battln Manchester Regmt		
War Diary	Arques	01/11/1917	01/11/1917
War Diary	Longue Croix	02/11/1917	09/11/1917
War Diary	Kinora M.Z.c.9.6	10/11/1917	11/11/1917
War Diary	Kempton M.14.b	12/11/1917	12/11/1917
War Diary	Scottish Lines A.23.5.5	13/11/1917	15/11/1917
War Diary	Montreal Camp H.19.b.4.7	16/11/1917	17/11/1917
War Diary	Montreal Camp	18/11/1917	19/11/1917
War Diary	Ypres	20/11/1917	22/11/1917
War Diary	Montreal Camp	23/11/1917	24/11/1917
War Diary	Berthen Area	25/11/1917	26/11/1917
War Diary	Caestre	27/11/1917	30/11/1917
Heading	Appendices And Casualty Return For November 1917 2/8 Battln Manchester Regmt		
Miscellaneous	2/8th Batt Manchester Regt		
Operation(al) Order(s)	2/8th Battalion Manchester Regiment Order No. 45	01/11/1917	01/11/1917
Operation(al) Order(s)	2/8th Battalion Manchester Regiment Order No. 46	08/11/1917	08/11/1917
Operation(al) Order(s)	2/8th Battalion Manchester Regiment Order No. 47	10/11/1917	10/11/1917
Operation(al) Order(s)	2/8th Batt Manchester Regt Order No. 48	11/11/1917	11/11/1917
Operation(al) Order(s)	2/8th Battalion Manchester Regiment Order No. 49	14/11/1917	14/11/1917

Operation(al) Order(s)	2/8th Batt Manchester Regt Order No. 50	18/11/1917	18/11/1917
Operation(al) Order(s)	2/8th Batt Manchester Regt Order No. 51	21/11/1917	21/11/1917
Operation(al) Order(s)	2/8th Battalion Manchester Regiment Order No. 52	23/11/1917	23/11/1917
Operation(al) Order(s)	2/8th Battalion Manchester Regiment Order No. 53	25/11/1917	25/11/1917
Map	Map		
Heading	2/8th Bn Manchester Regiment War Diary December 1917		
War Diary	Caestre	01/12/1917	16/12/1917
War Diary	Montreal Camp	17/12/1917	31/12/1917
Heading	2/8 Bn Manchester Regmt War Diary Appendices And Casualty Return For December 1917		
Operation(al) Order(s)	2/8th Batt Manchester Regiment Order No. 54	15/12/1917	15/12/1917
Operation(al) Order(s)	2/8th Battalion Manchester Regiment Order No. 55	30/12/1917	30/12/1917
Heading	2/8th Bn Manchester Regmt Appendices And Casualty Return For December 1917		
Miscellaneous	2/8th Bn Manchester Regt		
Miscellaneous	War Diary		
Heading	2/8 Bn Manchester Regmt War Diary For January 1918		
War Diary	Caestre	01/01/1918	11/01/1918
War Diary	Potijze	12/01/1918	12/01/1918
War Diary	Molenaerelsthoek J 4.b.80.55 Sheet 28 N.E.l.	13/01/1918	18/01/1918
War Diary	West Farm Camp I.10 Central	19/01/1918	22/01/1918
War Diary	Infantry Barracks Ypres	23/01/1918	28/01/1918
War Diary	Dash Crossing D17 C 50.90 Sheet 28 N.E.l.	29/01/1918	31/01/1918
Miscellaneous	Remarks On Tour		
Map	Map		
Heading	2/8 Bn Manchester Regmt Casualty Return for January 1918 Appendix I		
Miscellaneous	Casualties for month ending January 31st 1918		
Miscellaneous	2/8th Bn Manchester regt Casualties for month of January 1918		
Heading	2/8 Bn Manchester Regmt Operation Orders For January 1918		
Operation(al) Order(s)	2/9th Bn The Manchester Regiment Operation Order No. 56	09/01/1918	09/01/1918
Operation(al) Order(s)	2/9th Batt The Manchester Regiment Operation Order No. 55		
Operation(al) Order(s)	2/8th Bn Manchester Regt Order No. 56	09/01/1918	09/01/1918
Operation(al) Order(s)	2/8th Bn Manchester Regiment Order No. 57	10/01/1918	10/01/1918
Miscellaneous	Movement Table	11/01/1918	11/01/1918
Operation(al) Order(s)	2/8th Bn Manchester Regt Order No. 58	10/01/1918	10/01/1918
Operation(al) Order(s)	2/8th Battalion Manchester Regt Order No. 59	12/01/1918	12/01/1918
Operation(al) Order(s)	2/8th Bn Manchester Regiment Order No. 60	14/01/1918	14/01/1918
Operation(al) Order(s)	2/8th Batt Manchester Regt Order No. 61	17/01/1918	17/01/1918
Operation(al) Order(s)	2/8th Bn Manchester Regiment Order No. 62	21/01/1918	21/01/1918
Operation(al) Order(s)	2/8th Bn Manchester Regt Order No. 63	25/01/1918	25/01/1918
Heading	War Diary 2/8th Man. R. for Feb 1918 Vol 12		
War Diary	Left Sub Sector 66th Divisional Front	01/02/1918	02/02/1918
War Diary	Anzac Support Battn Left Bde 66th Divisional Front	03/02/1918	08/02/1918
War Diary	Reninghelst Area	09/02/1918	10/02/1918
War Diary	School Camp (Sheet 27 L.3.d)	11/02/1918	13/02/1918
Heading	2/8 Battalion Manchester Regt Casualty Return For Feb 1918		
Miscellaneous	2/8th Battalion Manchester Regt		
Heading	2/8 Battn Manchester Regt Operation Order For Feb 1918		

Operation(al) Order(s)	2/8th Batt Manchester Regiment Order No. 63	03/02/1918	03/02/1918
Operation(al) Order(s)	2/8th Batt Manchester Regt Order No. 37	10/02/1918	10/02/1918
Miscellaneous	2/8 Bn Manchester Regiment	02/02/1918	02/02/1918

WO/95/B145/34

2/6 Battalion Manchester Reg.

199TH INFY BDE

2-8TH BN MANCH REGT
~~MAR 1917 - FEB 1918~~

1915 SEP — 1916 FEB
1917 MAR — 1918 FEB

DISBANDED

Army Form C. 2118.

WAR DIARY
or
INTELLIGENCE SUMMARY.
(Erase heading not required.)

Instructions regarding War Diaries and Intelligence Summaries are contained in F.S. Regs., Part II and the Staff Manual respectively. Title pages will be prepared in manuscript.

Hour, Date, Place	Summary of Events and Information	Remarks and references to Appendices
2pm 14/3/17 BOULOGNE	Disembarked and proceeded to REST CAMP, OSTROHOVE	Army
10am 15/3/17 BOULOGNE	Entrained	Army
3.30pm 16/3/17 BÉTHUNE	Billeted in AREA Nº 1 - joined 199th INFANTRY BRIGADE.	Army
17/3/17 BÉTHUNE	In billets	Army
18/3/17 BÉTHUNE	In billets - 10 Officers and 100 O.R. attached to 251st TUNNELLING COY R.E. 10 Officers and 280 R.and.F. & Lewis Guns attached by 199th INFANTRY BRIGADE to relieve M.G. COY in CAMBRIN SECTOR	Army
19/3/17 ANNEQUIN	Relieved 1st Bn BEDFORDSHIRE 5 BEF.R. MEN in Sheltered R.E.35 RFFELS 665 GRPBRIN LEFT SECTOR	Army See APPENDIX I
20/3/17 ANNEQUIN	In billets - Working parties from a/o R.E. and M.T.M.B. Weather cold and wet. Lewis Gun party detached on 18/3/17 rejoined Unit at 10pm	Army
21/3/17 ANNEQUIN	In billets - Working parties found for R.E. and M.T.M.B.- Weather cold and wet.	Army
22/3/17 ANNEQUIN	In billets - Working parties found for R.E. and T.M.Bs. - Weather cold - some snow	Army
23/3/17 CAMBRIN LEFT SECTOR	Relieved 2/7 Bn MARCH R. - 3 Coys in FRONT LINE, 1 in SUPPORT - Situation normal. No casualties - Weather cold but fine	Army See APPENDIX II
24/3/17 CAMBRIN LEFT SECTOR	Situation normal. Casualties wounded O.R.2 - Weather cold and fine	Army
25/3/17 CAMBRIN LEFT SECTOR	Situation normal - Casualties killed O.R.1 wounded O.R.1 - Weather cold and fine	Army

Army Form C. 2118.

WAR DIARY
-of-
INTELLIGENCE SUMMARY.
(Erase heading not required.)

Instructions regarding War Diaries and Intelligence Summaries are contained in F.S. Regs., Part II. and the Staff Manual respectively. Title pages will be prepared in manuscript.

Hour, Date, Place		Summary of Events and Information	Remarks and references to Appendices
26/3/17	CAMBRIN LEFT SECTOR	Situation normal – Casualties wounded O.R. 2 – Weather cold & Snowy	
27/3/17	CAMBRIN LEFT SECTOR	2 Coys Relieved by 2/10th Br. MANCH R. – Relief complete at 4.30 pm. Enemy T.M. active. Casualties wounded O.R. 8	
	CAMBRIN (LEFT) LEFT SECTOR	Relieved 2/5th R. MANCH R. and 2 Coys in VILLAGE LINES (SUPPORT). Relief complete 6 p.m.	
	CAMBRIN (RIGHT) RIGHT SECTOR	Relieved 2 Coys 6th LEICESTERS and 2 Coys 7th LEICESTERS in SUPPORT LINE. Relief complete wiring at 2.7/28 March. Weather cold and very wet	See Appendix III
28/3/17	CAMBRIN SECTOR	In Support – Situation normal. No casualties. Weather cold and stormy.	fmg
29/3/17	CAMBRIN SECTOR	In Support – Situation normal – no casualties. Weather cold and stormy	fmg
30/3/17	CAMBRIN SECTOR	In Support – Situation normal – no casualties. Weather Snowy	fmg
31/3/17	CAMBRIN RIGHT	Relieved 2/5th MANCH R. 2 Coys in FRONT LINE, 1 Coy in SUPPORT – Relief complete at 3.30 pm. Situation normal – no casualties. Weather fine. Army	See Appendix IV

J. H. Beaton Lt. Col.

Vol 1

War Diary

of

2/8 Bn The Manchester Regt.

from March 4th to March 31st.

1917.

Volume 1.

Appendix
A. T.P.R's.
B. Operation Orders.
C. Casualty Returns
D. Maps.

Appendix "B"

Operation Orders.

SECRET.

2/8th Battalion Manchester Regt. Order No.1.

Ref - BETHUNE (Combined Sheet) 1/40000.

Copy No.9.
18/3/17.

1. The 199th Infantry Brigade will relieve the 15th Infantry Brigade on March 19th 1917 in the CAMBRIN Sector.

2. One Officer per Coy. and one NCO per Platoon of the 15th Brigade will remain with incoming units till March 20th (day following relief).

3. 2/8th Manchesters will relieve 1st BEDFORDSHIRE REGT (Reserve)

4. Guides on March 19th - One per platoon from 15th Brigade at rendezvous   (cross roads on BETHUNE - LA BASSE ROAD - between BEUVRY and ANNEQUIN.

5. All defence schemes, secret maps, aeroplane photos, trench stores, etc. will be taken over from units being relieved and receipts given.

6. Brigade Headquarters, 199th Infantry Brigade, will close at 12 noon on March 19th and open at the same hour at CHATEAU DES PRES (   )

7. The completion of relief will be reported at once by O.C.Coys. to Battalion Headquarters.

8. Transport, vide location table, will march in rear of the Battalion with the following personnel.
    Quartermaster.
    Pioneers.
    Butchers (2)
    Shoemaker Sergt.
    Regimental Quartermaster Sergt.
    Quartermaster Stores (3)
    Post Corporal.
    Coy. Quartermaster Sergts.

(Sgd) G.McDougall, Capt. & Adjt.
2/8th Batt.Manchester Regt.

Issued by Orderly
at 10-15 p.m.

Copy No.	
1.	Commanding Officer.
2	O.C. "A" Coy.
3	O.C. "B" Coy.
4	O.C. "C" Coy.
5	O.C. "D" Coy.
6	Quartermaster.
7	Medical Officer.
8	Transport Officer.
9	War Diary.
10	Filed.

Appendix I   by Lt Col J R Balfour CO

SECRET.

2/8th Batt. Manchester Regt. Order No. 2.

Copy No. 1
22/3/17.

RELIEF. 1. 2/8th MANCH R. will relieve 2/7th MANCH R to-morrow, 23rd inst. Relief to commence at 2 p.m.

GUIDES. 2. Guides will be provided, 1 Officer per Coy and 1 NCO per platoon, by outgoing Battalion. They will be at ANNEQUIN X ROADS at 12-30 p.m. One Guide will be provided for H.Q.

BILLETS. 3. One NCO per Coy. and Sergt. Bratt (representing H.Q. Coy.) will meet advance party of 2/7th MANCH R at ANNEQUIN X ROADS at 10 a.m. and guide them to billets.

ORDER OF ENTRY INTO TRENCHES. 4. "B" Coy. and 2 platoons "A" Coy. (garrisons of TOWERS and MOUNTAIN KEEPS) to move first.
"C" Coy. to move second.
"D" Coy. to move third.
"A" Coy – less 2 platoons – to move fourth.
H.Q. to move last.

STORES, etc. 5. All trench stores, maps, etc. will be taken over and receipts given.

EVACUATION OF BILLETS.
6. Billets must be left clean, and Billeting Distribution Lists rendered to Orderly Room by 9 am.

BLANKETS & OFFICERS KITS. 7. The Transport Officer will place transport to convey these to Q.M. Stores at 10 a.m.

COOKERS. 8. The Transport Officer will send horses to remove these to Transport Lines at 1 p.m.

MEALS. 9. O.C. Coys. will arrange for a hot meal at 11-30 am.

COMPLETION OF RELIEF. 10. To be reported by "B.A.B" Code.

11. Acknowledge.

ISSUED AT 10 am. BY ORDERLIES.
Copy No. 1. Retained.
  "   " 2. 199th Bde.
  "   " 3. 2/7th Manch. R.
  "   " 4. C.O.
  "   " 5. 2nd in Comd.
  "   " 6. Adjutant.
  "   " 7. O.C. "A" Coy.
  "   " 8. O.C. "B" Coy.
  "   " 9. O.C. "C" Coy.
  "   " 10. O.C. "D" Coy.
  "   " 11. Transport Officer.
  "   " 12. Quartermaster.
  "   " 13. Medical Officer.

G McDougall
Capt. & Adjt.
2/8th Batt. Manchester Regt.

Appendix III   by Lt Col J.E. Balfour Cdg

RELIEF.   1/8th Batt. Manchester Regt. Order No. 3.
                            ───

Ref. Sheet 36c.N.W.1/10000.   Copy No. 21.
& BETHUNE (combined sheet) 1/40000.   27/3/17.

INFORMATION.   1. The Battalion will be relieved by the 2/10th
                    Batt. Manchester Regt. to-day.

GUIDES.   2. Each O.C.Coy. will detail one guide to be at the
                    junction of HARLEY STREET – LA BASSEE ROAD A 30 d 24
                    at 8-15 a.m. to guide the Coy. Signallers and Lewis
                    Gunners of the 2/10th Manchesters. These will proceed
                    via THE LANE.

                    The Sniping Officer will detail 2 guides and the
                    Signalling Officer one guide for Snipers and Headquarters
                    Signallers. These will proceed via MAISON ROUGE.

                    Each O.C.Coy. will furnish guides consisting of
                    1 Officer per Coy. and 1 N.C.R. per platoon to be at
                    the junction of HARLEY STREET & LA BASSEE ROAD at
                    9 o'clock.

                    The 2/10th Manchesters will be led in via the
                    LANE in the following order.
                        1st. 2 platoons of Support Coy. for 12 HURST KEEP
                              and OLD BOOTS TRENCH.
                        2nd. Right Firing Line Company.
                        3rd. Central Firing Line Company.
                        4th. 1 platoon of Support Company to TOWERS RESERVE
                              TRENCH.
                        5th. Left Firing Line Company.
                        6th. 1 platoon Support Company for MOUNTAIN KEEP.

MAPS, etc.   3. All Defence Schemes, Secret Maps, Aeroplane Photos,
                    Trench Stores, etc. will be handed over to relieving
                    units, and receipts taken.

**COMPLETION   4. Will be immediately reported to Battalion H.Q.
OF RELIEF.**   by B.A.R. Code.

                    On completion of relief by 2/10th Manchesters
                    Companies will proceed as follows, and in the order
                    laid down :—
                        2 platoons "A" Coy. via OLD BOOTS TRENCH to relieve
                    2 platoons 2/5th Manchesters VILLAGE LINE, CAMBRIN
                    RIGHT SUB-SECTOR. Guide will be met at junction of
                    MAISON ROUGE and WIMPOLE TRENCH A 36 b 56.40 at
                    12 noon.
                        "D" Coy. – less 1 platoon – via OLD BOOTS TRENCH
                    as follows :—
                        3 platoons to relieve 1 Coy. 7th Leicesters
                    in RAILWAY RESERVE TRENCH.
                        1 platoon to relieve 1 Coy. 5th Leicesters
                    in CENTRAL KEEP.
                        Guides will be met at junction of RAILWAY
                    ALLEY and OLD BOOTS G 4 b 65.30 at 1 pm.
                        "C" Coy. via OLD BOOTS TRENCH to relieve 1 Coy.
                    5th Leicesters in RESERVE TRENCH. Guide will be
                    met at junction of RAILWAY ALLEY and OLD BOOTS
                    G 4 b 65.30 at 1 pm.
                        "B" Coy. via MAISON ROUGE to relieve 1 Coy.
                    2/5th Manchesters in VILLAGE LINE CAMBRIN RIGHT
                    SUB-SECTOR. Guide will be met at junction of
                    MAISON ROUGE and WIMPOLE TRENCH A 36 b 56.40 at
                    12 noon.
                        2 platoons "A" Coy. via OLD BOOTS TRENCH to
                    relieve 2 platoons 2/5th Manchesters VILLAGE LINE
                    CAMBRIN RIGHT SUB-SECTOR. Guide will be met at
                    junction of MAISON ROUGE and WIMPOLE TRENCH A 36 b 56.40
                    at 12 noon.
                        Headquarters Personnel will proceed via MAISON
                    ROUGE – ANNEQUIN to New Headquarters, RAILWAY
                    HOUSE, ANNEQUIN CHURCH, L 5 b 60.

                                                           A.T.O.

1 platoon of "D" Coy. will leave the trenches at 8-30 and proceed via MAISON ROUGE - ANNEQUIN to VERMELLE, where they will meet guide of 7th Leicesters at CLARKE KEEP G 8 a 65.30. This platoon will relieve 1 Coy. of the 7th Leicesters in LANCASHIRE TRENCH.

MAPS, etc. 5. All Defence Schemes, Secret Maps, Aeroplane Photos, Trench Stores, etc. will be taken over from Units being relieved, and receipts given.

COMPLETION OF RELIEF. 6. On completion of relief O.C. Coys. will immediately send in a Disposition Return showing their Headquarters, with map references. Completion of relief will be reported at once to Battalion Headquarters by B.A.B. code, or by runner if telephonic communication is not available.

(Signed) G. McDougall.

Capt. & Adjt.
2/6th Battalion Manchester Regt.

ISSUED AT 2 A.M.
Copies to
No.1 Headquarters 199th Inf.Bgde.
No.2. O.C. 2/6th Batt.Manchester Regt.
No.3. 2nd in Command.   do.
No.4. Adjutant   do.
No.5. O.C. "A" Coy.
No.6. "   "B" Coy.
No.7. "   "C" Coy.
No.8. "   "D" Coy.
No.9. " 2/5th Manchester Regt.
No.10. " 2/6th   do.
No.11. " 2/7th   do.
No.12. " 6th Bn.Leicester Regt.
No.13. " 7th   do.
No.14. " 2/10th Bn.Manchester Regt.
No.15. " Sniping Officer.
No.16. " Transport Officer.
No.17. " Signalling Officer.
No.18. " Lewis Gun Officer.
No.19. " Quartermaster.
No.20. Medical Officer.
No.21. War Diary.
No.22. Filed.

Appendix IV

SECRET.   Copy No.13.

2/7th Battalion Manchester Regiment Order No.6.
                                        30/3/17.

1. RELIEF.   The Battalion will be relieved in the
                  trenches on the morning of the 31st
                  inst. by the 2/8th Bn. Manchester Regt.
                  and will proceed into support.

2. DISPOSITION   "A" Coy.   VILLAGE LINE, RIGHT SECTOR
   OF BATTALION   "B" Coy.   RIGHT RESERVE TRENCH.
   IN SUPPORT.   "C" Coy.   Two Platoons in RAILWAY
                             RESERVE TRENCH
                             One Platoon in CENTRAL
                             KEEP.
                             One Platoon in LANCASHIRE
                             TRENCH.
                  "D" Coy.   VILLAGE LINE, LEFT SECTOR
                  "D" Coy. will not move back until
                  11-30 a.m.

3. ROUTE.   In accordance with attached Route Table.

4. HANDING   All trench stores, maps, defence schemes
   OVER.   etc. will be handed over to the
                  incoming unit. Receipts will be obtained.

5. TUNNELS   All Tunns dug-outs, cookhouses and
   & DUG-   latrines, will be left scrupulously
   OUTS.   clean.

6. DETAILS.   Stretcher Bearers, water duty men,
                  sanitary men and three signallers will
                  remain with their Companies, and be
                  rationed by them while in Support.

7. REPORT   By BAB Code as soon as complete.
   OF RELIEF.

8.   ACKNOWLEDGE.
                              (Sgd) J.A.Schofield, Capt.
   Issued at 2-30pm.   Adjt.2/7th Bn.Manchester Regt.

Copy No.1. Retained.
     2. 199th Bde.
     3. C.O.
     4. Adjt.
     5. 2nd in Command.
     6. O.C. "A" Coy.
     7. O.C. "B" Coy.
     8. O.C. "C" Coy.
     9. O.C. "D" Coy.
    10. O.C. "H.Q." Coy.
    11. O.C. 2/8th Manch.R.
    12.   -do-
    13.   -do-
    14.   -do-
    15.   -do-
    16.   -do-
    17. R.S.M.
    18. Q.M.
    19. M.O.
    20. War Diary.

SECRET

Time Table and Routes on March 31st. RELIEF DAY.

Relief of CAMBRIN RIGHT 2/4th MANCHESTERS BY 2/8th MANCHESTERS.

-- GUIDES --

RELIEF OF	COY.	BY.	TIME	AT.	ROUTE	COMPLETE BY.
LEFT FIRING LINE.	"A" COY 2/4TH	"D" COY 2/8	9-0 A.M.	JUNCTION RESERVE & QUARRY ALLEY	RY RESERVE TRENCH - QUARRY ALLEY	2-0 P.M.
CENTRE FIRING LINE.	"B" COY 2/4TH	"A" COY 2/8	9-0 A.M.	" LANCASHIRE TRY & QUARRY ALLEY, RESERVE TR. LEFT BOYAU. (WINDY CORNER)	QUARRY ALLEY	2-0 P.M.
RIGHT FIRING LINE.	"C" COY 2/4TH.	"C" COY 2/8TH	9-0 A.M.	SAVILLE ROW & RESERVE TRS.	SAVILLE ROW	2-0 P.M.
RIGHT SUPPORT LINE	"C" COY 2/8TH	"B" COY 2/8TH	10-0 A.M.	LANCASHIRE TRENCH & QUARRY ALLEY, QUARRY ALLEY & RESERVE TR.		2-0 P.M.
LEFT SUPPORT LINE	"D" COY 2/4TH	"B" COY 2/7	9-0 A.M.		LEFT BOYAU	2-0 P.M.

NOTE

(1) Situation of H.Q. Coy. 2/4TH BN. MAN. R. will be ANNEQUIN FOSSE.

(2) Companies of the 2/8TH BN. MAN R. will each leave a representative to hand over SUPPORT LINE to Companies of the 2/4th BN. MAN. R.

Appendix "C"

Casualty Returns.

	Casualties.		Accidental.	
Date.	Killed.	Wounded.	Killed.	Wounded.
24.3.17.	1.	2.		
25.3.17.	1.	1.		
26.3.17.		2.		
27.3.17.		8.		

APPENDIX B

MAPS.

CONFIDENTIAL

War Diary

of

2/8" Bn Manchester Regiment

from 1st April 1917 to 30" April 1917

Volume I

Army Form C. 2118.

WAR DIARY
or
INTELLIGENCE SUMMARY.
(Erase heading not required.)

Instructions regarding War Diaries and Intelligence Summaries are contained in F.S. Regs., Part II. and the Staff Manual respectively. Title pages will be prepared in manuscript.

Hour, Date, Place	Summary of Events and Information	Remarks and references to Appendices
1-4-17 CAMBRIN RIGHT.	Situation normal – Casualties killed OR 2 wounded OR 5 including 3 S.S./unfitted (rifle) – weather fine	Army
2-4-17 CAMBRIN RIGHT.	Enemy T.M.'s active during night & blew in mouth of tunnel, cutting off Observer at G.4. A.8.3. Casualties killed OR 4 wounded OR 4. Weather wet and snowy.	See MAP "A". Army
3-4-17 CAMBRIN RIGHT.	Repair to tunnel completed at 12.30pm. Enemy trench mortar active during night (3"/4") Casualties wounded OR 2. Listening post missing OR 1 (Smothered) – weather wet	Army
4-4-17 CAMBRIN RIGHT.	Enemy T.M.'s active up to 6 a.m. Casualties killed OR 3 wounded OR 4. making OR 1 (Smothered) Relieved by 2/7 MANCH R & went into billets making OR 1 (Smothered) at NOYELLES – Weather fine.	Army
5-4-17 NOYELLES.	In Reserve. Weather showery	Army
6-4-17 do	do	Army
7-4-17 do	do	Army
8-4-17 do	do	Army
9-4-17 CAMBRIN RIGHT.	Relieved 2/7 MANCH R in CAMBRIN RIGHT – Relief complete at 2.30 pm.	See APPENDIX "A". Army
10-4-17 do	Situation normal – Weather fine.	Army
11-4-17 do	do	Army
12-4-17 do	Casualties killed OR 1 wounded OR 1 (accidentally (bayonet)) – Weather cold & showery. Somewhat	Army
	Relieved by 2/7 "MANCH R. Relief complete at 1.30pm. Casualties wounded OR 1. Things have not been much in evidence. At enemy trench mortars were in action also during the previous tour. On relief of the Battalion went into Support – 2 Coys CAMBRIN RIGHT – 2 Coys CAMBRIN LEFT. H.Q. FOSSE HOUSE, ANNEQUIN.	See APPENDIX "A". Army

Army Form C. 2118.

WAR DIARY
INTELLIGENCE SUMMARY.
(Erase heading not required.)

Instructions regarding War Diaries and Intelligence Summaries are contained in F.S. Regs., Part II and the Staff Manual respectively. Title pages will be prepared in manuscript.

2

Hour, Date, Place		Summary of Events and Information	Remarks and references to Appendices
13-4-17	CAMBRIN SECTOR	In Support - Weather warmer & fine	Army
14-4-17	do	do - Casualties wounded O.R.1. weather fine.	Army
15-4-17	do	do	Army
16-4-17	do	Weather wet.	
17-4-17	CAMBRIN RIGHT	Relieved 2/7" MANCH. R. in CAMBRIN RIGHT. Relief comp. abt 2:30pm	See Appendix A 3
		Situation normal. Casualties wounded O.R.1. weather wet.	Army
18-4-17	do	Situation normal. Casualties wounded O.R.1. weather wet.	Army
19-4-17	do	do Casualties Killed O.R.1 wounded O.R.1. weather wet.	Army
20-4-17	do	do Weather wet	Army
		Relieved by 2/7" MANCH R. The weather was very quiet 8am similar to the last 2	See Appendix A 4
		The weather was very wet though there was little to relieve in a water logged
		condition. Completion for 20 April wounded O.R. 2. Un relief felt
		Battalion went into Brigade Reserve at NOYELLES.
21-4-17	NOYELLES	In Brigade Reserve. Weather fine	Army
22-4-17	do	do	Army
23-4-17	do	do	Army
24-4-17	do	At 8:30pm left NOYELLES + came upon relief of	see MAP 2
		71st Inf Bde. relieving 9" NORFOLKS in ST ELIE RIGHT SECTION.	+ Appendix A 5
		In O.R.order to Trammeling Camp on 1/3/17 regiment making Trench Strength
		about 5200 R.
25-4-17	ST ELIE RIGHT	Situation normal. Weather fine.	Army
26-4-17	ST ELIE RIGHT	At 10 a.m. command of section passed from 71st Inf Bde. to 16" Inf Bde.	Army
		Situation normal. Casualties wounded 2/Lt. F. COLLIER. weather fine	Army

Army Form C. 2118.

WAR DIARY

3 / INTELLIGENCE SUMMARY

(Erase heading not required.)

Instructions regarding War Diaries and Intelligence Summaries are contained in F.S. Regs., Part II and the Staff Manual respectively. Title pages will be prepared in manuscript.

Hour, Date, Place	Summary of Events and Information	Remarks and references to Appendices
29/4/17. ST ELIE RIGHT.	Situation normal. Casualties O.R.1. weather fine.	
29/4/17 ST ELIE RIGHT.	4 a.m. Enemy patrol 1 Officer 20 O.R. tried to enter our trenches near BOYAU 78. but were driven off by our front-seds, capturing 1 who died (?) unwounded prisoner. Enemy Artillery heavily bombarded Support Trenches about G.17.c.50.05 with 4.2" & 5.9". Also communications in rear. Casualties Rifles O.R. 3 wounded O.R. 10. weather fine & warm.	Army
29/4/17. ST ELIE RIGHT.	Situation normal. Casualties Rifles O.R.1. wounded O.R. 1.	
30/4/17 ST ELIE RIGHT.	Situation normal. Casualties wounded O.R. 3 (including 1 accidentally (very light)) Weather fine. During the whole of the tour the enemy Artillery was very active particularly on communications in rear of Front line.	Army

J.R. Bayzon? Lt.Col.
Cmdg 3/6 Manchester Rgt.
2/5/17

WAR DIARY
INTELLIGENCE SUMMARY

(Erase heading not required.)

Army Form C. 2118.

Instructions regarding War Diaries and Intelligence Summaries are contained in F. S. Regs., Part II. and the Staff Manual respectively. Title pages will be prepared in manuscript.

Hour, Date, Place	Summary of Events and Information	Remarks and references to Appendices
2.5.17. NOYELLES	Relieved by the 8th Bn. Bedfordshire Regt. Relay Completed by 2.30 A.M. Battalion in Bde. Reserve. Weather fine. Casualties O.R. 2 Killed	EvC
3.5.17 NOYELLES	Bde. Reserve – Casualties nil. Weather fine.	EvC.
4.5.17 NOYELLES	Bde. Reserve – Shelled during the afternoon – Weather fine. Casualties OR 6 Wounded.	EvC.
5.5.17 NOYELLES	Bde. Reserve – Weather fine – Casualties – OR 1 nil	EvC
6.6.17. (Sunday) CAMBRIN Reylt.	Relieved the 2/5th Manchester Regt. Relief Completed by 11 am. Situation quiet. Weather fine. Casualties OR Nil.	EvC see Appendix A 1
7.5.17 CAMBRIN Right	Situation normal. Weather fine. Casualties OR 5 Wounded)	EvC.
8.5.17 CAMBRIN Right	Situation exceptionally quiet all day night Weather fine – Casualties , Officers – (Capt. Williams Shell Shock) OR. 2.	EvC
9.5.17 CAMBRIN Right	Situation normal. 6.30 a.m. 3 put up heavy barrage on M.P.O. Point 7.30 pm Weather fine, Casualties OR	EvC.
10.5.17 CAMBRIN Right	Situation quiet. 1 M.G. on Right Coy but suspected on right. Shots taken and caused death to one – Weather fine – Casualties by T.M. Weather fine Casualties OR 1 wounded). AN	EvC
11.5.17 CAMBRIN Right	Situation very quiet. Our T.M's doing successful work in Kelverhound Trench Casualties OR 3 wounded.	EvC

WAR DIARY
INTELLIGENCE SUMMARY
(Erase heading not required.)

Army Form C. 2118.

Hour, Date, Place	Summary of Events and Information	Remarks and references to Appendices
12.5.17. CAMBRIN Right	Situation Quiet - Relieved by the 2/I Manc Regt. Relief Completed at 12 Noon. "B" Bn in Support - "B. Coy. Reserve line - "C" Central Keep. "D" Cambrin Chantraw. Weather fine - Casualties OR 1 killed.	Esse See Appendix A 2
13 to 18. 5.17 "B" in Support -	The last 6 days have been exceptionally quiet - T.M.'s Artillery Rifle Grenades, quite below normal. The weather has also been good - very fine. Casualties Considerably less.	Esse
18. 5.17 CAMBRIN Right	Very quiet during tour in Support. Heaters very Quiet. Cavaliers the Battn. Relieved by 2/7 Buffs Regt. Relief Completed by 1.15 am. Ration Ketch Cavaliers Rite.	Esse
19.5.17 CAMBRIN Right	Situation Normal - Several shelling in Quarry, on MTM Quarry Alley about 2.5.5.9. Morning out one MTM. Weather fine - Casualties OR one Wounded.	Esse
20.5.17 CAMBRIN Right	Situation Quiet - Weather Keeps this Cambrin Rite on Cambrin	Esse

Army Form C. 2118.

WAR DIARY
INTELLIGENCE SUMMARY.
(Erase heading not required.)

Instructions regarding War Diaries and Intelligence Summaries are contained in F.S. Regs., Part II. and the Staff Manual respectively. Title pages will be prepared in manuscript.

Hour, Date, Place	Summary of Events and Information	Remarks and references to Appendices
21.5.17 CAMBRIN RYLT.	Situation quiet. Barrage on W&D Point. Weather fine. Cambrin O.R. 4 Wounded 2 Killed	Evse
22.5.17 Cambrin Ry Lt.	Situation normal. Barrage fire. 6" high explos. on left sector. Bombs thrown from enemy trench. NORTHAMPTON Retaliates. Weather showery. Cambrin O.R. 1 wounded	Evse
23.5.17 Cambrin Ry.I.T.	Increased enemy T.M activity. Shells falling short of Northampton trench. 69d ST57 – left B.T.M. G4A 6015 – Cambrin O.R. nil. Weather fine. Early barrage.	Evse
24.5.17 Cambrin Ry.I.T.	Situation normal. Weather fine. Cambrin O.R. 5 wounded, includn. 2 Bty officers.	Evse.
25.5.17 Cambrin Ry.I.T.	Heavy shelling vf FOSSE 8. Left Borgau – again Shells – Weather fine. Cambrin O.R. 1 killed, 1 wounded.	Evse
26.5.17 CAMBRIN Ry.I.T.	Situation normal. Weather fine. Casualties O.R. 1 killed 4 wounded.	Evse.
27.5.17 to NOYELLES.	Relieved by the 2/1st N/c Regt. troops on the left b/s/4th Regt. proceeded to NOYELLES – Reft. front	See Appendix A 5
1.6.17 NOYELLES.	"B" "C" Coys between the 2/5th/c Regt in Cambrin. Left. Cambrin nil. Weather bright	See Appendix A 6

Vol 3

Confidential

War Diary
of
2/8th Bn. Manchester Regiment.

from 1st May 1917 to 31st May 1917.

(Volume I)

Appendices

Appendix A.

Operation Orders

SECRET.   Appendix B 1.

2/8th Batt. MANCHESTER REGIMENT ORDER No. 11.

                                                  Copy No.......
                                                  5/8/17.

1. The Battalion will relieve 2/5th MANCH.R. in
   CAMBRIN LEFT SECTOR to-morrow.

2. Time & Route Table attached.

3. The VERMELLES - ANNEQUIN ROAD is NOT to be used
   by any troops, and all now sent will be via PHILOSOPHE.

4. Greatcoats will NOT be taken into the trenches.
   Greatcoats and packs to be dumped ready for loading
   at 8 p.m. to-day
   Officers' kits to be dumped ready for loading at 8 p.m. on
   to-morrow.

5. No parties larger than platoons at 300 yards distance
   distance will move on relief. In exposed places, where
   it is necessary owing to lack of communication trenches
   to move in the open, movement will be by sections.

6. Receipts will be given for all trench stores, maps, etc.
   taken over, and copies forwarded to Batt. H.Q. by 5 p.m.
   on day of relief.

7. Disposition reports with sketches will be forwarded to
   reach Batt. H.Q. by 4 p.m. on day of relief.

8. All hutments to be left scrupulously clean.

9. Completion of Relief to be reported by BAB Code.

10. ACKNOWLEDGE.

                           (Sgd) G. McDougall, Capt. & Adjt.
                                 2/8th Batt. Manchester Regt.

Issued at 5-20 pm.

Copy No. 1.....199th Inf. Bgde.
  "   " 2   2/5th MANCH.R.
  "   " 3.   2/6th   do.
  "   " 4.   2/7th   do.
  "   " 5   O.C. "A" Coy.
  "   " 6   O.C. "B" Coy.
  "   " 7   O.C. "C" Coy.
  "   " 8   O.C. "D" Coy.
  "   " 9   O.C. "H.Q." Coy.
  "   " 10   R.S.M.
  "   " 11   M.O.
  "   " 12   T.O. & Q.M.
  "   " 13/14   War Diary.

Time and Route Table.

Relief of 2/5th Manchester Regt. by 2/8th Batt. Manchester Regt. on 6/5/17.

Relief of.	Coy.	by	Coy.	Starting Time.	Route.
Right Firing Line.	D.Coy.2/5th M.R.	A.Coy.	2/8th	7 am.	GORDON ALLEY BARTS ALLEY SAVILLE ROW.
Centre Firing Line.	B.Coy.	do.	D.Coy.	do.	7-30 am.	QUARRY ALLEY LEFT BOYAU.
Left Firing Line.	C.Coy.	do.	C.Coy.	do.	7 am.	QUARRY ALLEY.
Right Reserve.	A.Coy.	do	B.Coy.	do.	7-30 am.	GORDON ALLEY. BARTS ALLEY.

Notes. Firing Line Coys. will send day garrisons of posts in advance, under one Officer per Coy. They will leave NOYELLES one hour in advance of the remainder of their Coys. and proceed by above mentioned routes.
Day garrison for No.19 post will meet a guide of 2/5th Manch.R. at Junction of RESERVE TRENCH and QUARRY ALLEY at 7 a.m. and will be led to their position via BOYAU 2.

APPENDIX A 2

SECRET.

Copy No 13

2/7th MANCHESTER REGIMENT ORDER No 12

11/5/17

1. The Battalion will be relieved by 2/7's MANCH R tomorrow, 12th May 1917.

2. On relief the Battalion will go into Support, CAMBRIN SECTOR.

3. Route and Time Table attached.

4. No parties larger than platoons at 300 yards distance will move on relief. In exposed places where it is necessary owing to lack of communication trenches to move in the open, movement will be by sections only.

5. Receipts will be taken for all maps, trench stores &c handed over & a copy forwarded to Battalion H.Q. by 10 a.m. on the morning after relief.

6. Trenches, dug-outs, kitchens &c are to be left clean.

7. Battalion H.Q will be at F.29.a.8.8.

8 Completion of relief to be reported by
BAB CODE.

9 Acknowledge

G McDougall
Capt & Adjt

Issued at 8.30pm.   2/8" Bn MANCH R

Copy No 1   199" I.B.
        2   2/5" MANCH R
        3   2/6" MANCH R
        4   2/7" MANCH R
        5   O.C A Coy
        6   O.C B Coy
        7   O.C C Coy
        8   O.C D Coy
        9   O.C H.Q Coy
        10   M.O
        11   G.M.T.O
        12   R.S.M.
        13   War Diary
        14   do.

7

Relief Table – May 12th 1917

Relief of	Coy	by	Coy	Time	present to	Route
1 Right F.L	A Coy 2/8 Manch R		C Coy 2/5 Manch R	2pm	RIGHT SUPPORT / CAMBRIN LEFT	SAVILLE ROW, BART'S ALLEY, LANCASHIRE TRENCH
2 Centre F.L	D Coy	"	B	2.30pm	LEFT SUPPORT / CAMBRIN LEFT	LEFT BOYAU, RESERVE TRENCH, BART'S ALLEY
3 Left F.L	C Coy	"	D	2pm	REAR SUPPORT / CAMBRIN RIGHT	LANCASHIRE TRENCH, VILLAGE LINE
4 Right Support	B Coy	"	A	2.30pm	LEFT SUPPORT / CAMBRIN RIGHT	QUARRY ALLEY, RAILWAY RESERVE TRENCH

NOTE. Each Coy will send advance party of 1 Offr & 2 NCOs per platoon at 10am to take over new position from 2/5 Manch R.

APPENDIX A 3

SECRET.

2/8th Batt. MANCHESTER REGT. ORDER No.13.

Copy No. ....
17/5/17.

1. The Battalion will relieve the 2/7th MANCH R. in CAMBRIN RIGHT to-morrow, May 18th 1917.

2. Route and Time Table attached.

3. No parties larger than platoons at 300 yards distance will move in relief.

4. Receipts will be given for all maps, trench stores, etc. taken over, and copies forwarded to Batt.H.Q. by 6 p.m. on day of relief.

5. Billets, trenches, dug-outs, etc. must be left clean.

6. Completion of relief to be immediately reported by B.A.B.Code.

7. Acknowledge.

G M Dougall
Capt. & Adjt.
2/8th Batt. Manchester Regt.

Issued at 9-30 p.m.

Copy No. 1   1 8th Inf. Bde.
do.   2   2/8th MANCH.R.
do.   3   2/9th   do.
do.   4   2/7th   do.
do.   5   O.C. "A" Coy.
do.   6   O.C. "B" Coy.
do.   7   O.C. "C" Coy.
do.   8   O.C. "D" Coy.
do.   9   O.C. "H.Q." Coy.
do. 10   Medical Officer.
do. 11   Transport Officer & Q.M.
do. 12   R.S.M.
do. 13/14 War Diary.

RELIEF TABLE — MAY 18th 191_

RELIEF OF	Coy	BY Coy	STARTING TIME	ROUTE
1. RIGHT FIRING LINE	"C" Coy 21st Manch'r	"A" Coy 18th Manch.	8·30 a.m.	RAILWAY ALLEY — QUARRY ALLEY — RESERVE TRENCH — S.P. 3.
2. CENTRE FIRING LINE	"B" Coy.	—do—	8·30 a.m.	RAILWAY ALLEY — QUARRY ALLEY — LEFT BOYAU
3. LEFT FIRING LINE	"D" Coy.	"B" Coy. —do—	8 a.m.	QUARRY ALLEY
4. RIGHT SUPPORT	"A" Coy.	"C" Coy. —do—	9·30 a.m.	

Notes:— Each Coy will leave 1 Officer to hand over to incoming unit.

H.Q. Coy will move at 8·30 a.m.

Relief to be completed by 12 noon.

APPENDIX A4

SECRET.

1/8th Batt. MANCHESTER REGIMENT Order No.14.

Copy No. 8
3/5/17.

1. "C" Coy. will relieve "A" Coy. in the Right Firing Line at 10 A.M. to-morrow, May 4th 1917.

2. On relief, "A" Coy. will take up the position vacated by "C" Coy. in SUPPORT.

3. Receipts will be given for all maps, stores, etc. taken over.

4. Relief to be completed by 12 noon.

5. Completion of relief to be reported by R.A.B. Code.

6. Acknowledge.

H McDougall
Capt. & Adjt.
1/8th Batt. Manchester Regiment.

Issued at 7 P.M.

Copy No. 1... 10 th Inf. Bde.
"   "   2... O.C. "A" Coy
"   "   3... O.C. "B" Coy.
"   "   4... O.C. "C" Coy.
"   "   5... O.C. "D" Coy.
"   "   6... Transport Officer.
"   "   7... R.S.M.
"   "   8... War Diary.
"   "   9...   do.

APPENDIX A 5.

SECRET.

2/8th Bn. MANCHESTER REGT. Order No.15.

Copy No. 14
26/5/17.

1. The Battalion will be relieved by 2/7th MANCH R. in CAMBRIN RIGHT to-morrow, May 27th 1917.

2. On being relieved the Battalion will proceed into Reserve Hutments at NOYELLES.

3. Route and Time Table attached.

4. No parties larger than Platoons at 300 yds. distance will move on relief. In exposed places, or where it is necessary through lack of communication trenches to move in the open, movement will be by sections only.

5. Receipts will be taken for all maps, documents, trench stores, etc. handed over.

6. All trenches, dugouts, cookhouses and latrines must be left clean.

7. Completion of relief to be reported by BAB Code.

8. Acknowledge.

G. McDougall
Capt. & Adjt.
2/8th Batt. Manchester Regt.

Issued at 6-30 pm.

Copy No.1.	199th Inf. Bde.
" " 2.	2/5th MANCH R.
" " 3.	2/8th do.
" " 4.	2/7th do.
" " 5.	O.C. "A" Coy.
" " 6.	" "B" "
" " 7.	" "C" "
" " 8.	" "D" "
" " 9.	" H.Q. "
" "10.	M.O.
" "11.	T.O. & Q.M.
" "12.	R.S.M.
" "13/14.	War Diary.

RELIEF TABLE. — May 27th 1917.

Relief of.	2/8 MANCH.R. Coy.	by 2/7 MANCH.R. Coy.	Starting Time of Relieving Coy.	Route of exit of Relieved Coy.
RIGHT FIRING LINE.	"C" Coy.	"C" Coy.	9 a.m.	SAVILLE ROW – BARTS ALLEY – GORDON ALLEY.
CENTRE FIRING LINE.	"D" Coy.	"A" Coy.	9 a.m.	LEFT BOYAU – QUARRY ALLEY – VERMELLES.
LEFT FIRING LINE.	"B" Coy.	"D" Coy.	9 a.m.	QUARRY ALLEY RESERVE TRENCH BARTS ALLEY GORDON ALLEY
RIGHT SUPPORT.	"A" Coy.	"B" Coy.	9-30 am.	BARTS ALLEY GORDON ALLEY.

Note :- H.Q. will leave the trenches by GORDON ALLEY.

Appendix A 6

SECRET.

2/8th Batt. MANCHESTER REGIMENT ORDER No.13.

Copy No. 6
1/6/17.

1. "B" and "C" Companies 2/8th MANCH. R. will relieve "C" and "D" Companies, 2/5th MANCH. R. in CAMBRIN LEFT on night of June 1st/2nd 1917.

2. A guide from 2/5th MANCH. R. will meet the head of Relief Companies at the junction of MUNSTER PARADE and RAILWAY ALLEY at 10 p.m.

3. Receipts will be given for all trench stores, etc. taken over.

4. Completion of relief will be reported by B.A.B.Code.

       (Signed) G. McDougall, Capt. & Adjt.
       2/8th Batt. Manchester Regt.

Issued at 8-30 p.m.

Copy No. 1. Retained.
" " 2. 199th Inf. Bgde.
" " 3. 2/5th MANCH. R.
" " 4. O.C. "B" Coy. 2/8th MANCH. R.
" " 5. O.C. "C" Coy. 2/8th MANCH. R.
" " 6/7. War Diary.

Confidential

War Diary
of
2/8th Bn. Manchester Regiment

from 1st June 1917 to 30th June 1917.

(Volume 1)

WAR DIARY or INTELLIGENCE SUMMARY

(Erase heading not required.)

Army Form C. 2118.

Instructions regarding War Diaries and Intelligence Summaries are contained in F. S. Regs., Part II. and the Staff Manual respectively. Title pages will be prepared in manuscript.

Hour, Date, Place	Summary of Events and Information	Remarks and references to Appendices
2.6.17. NOYELLES. "B" & "C" Coys. CAMBRIN. Left.	Situation normal. Weather fine. Casualties on night of 1/2nd June 1/5th "B" & "C" Coys relieved 2 Coys of 1/5th W.R. Regt in CAMBRIN. Right.	Estd. See appendix A.1. See appendix B.1.
3.6.17. NOYELLES. "B" & "D" Coys. CAMBRIN. Left.	"C" Coy relieved "A" "D" Coy. Situation normal in Brigade Reserve. Situation normal. Casualties O.R. 6 Wounded, 3 killed. Weather fine.	B.H.Q. See appendix A.2.
4.6.17. NOYELLES	"B" Coy relieved by detachment of K.L. own Regt Cavalry. "B" NOYELLES Battalion in Brigade Reserve. Weather fine. Casualties Nil.	B.H.Q. See appendix A.3.
5.6.17. CAMBRIN. Right	"D" Coy in CAMBRIN Rt. left - relieved by one company of 3/6 B. Fusiliers Regt. "D" Coy relieved to NOYELLES. 6 am. Other 3 Coys relieved the 2/4 3rd B. Fusiliers Regt. in CAMBRIN Right. Relief complete by 12 mid-night. Situation during some of night quiet. Casualties - Nil.	See appendix A.4, A.5 + B.1. B.H.Q.
6.6.17. CAMBRIN. Right	Situation normal on left night firing lines, Bursts of intense fire. activity on centre firing line. Spoil Heap in NORTH M1070s TR - N0.6 Post - G.16.C.25.50. Badly damaged by minnies. Weather fine. Casualties O.R. 3 Wounded.	See appendix B.2. B.H.Q.
7.6.17. CAMBRIN. Right	Situation normal. Weather Unsettled. Casualties O.R. 3 wounded, 1 duly inflicted.	B.H.Q.
8.6.17. CAMBRIN. Right	Situation normal. Wet. 8.30 pm. Blew a party of 7 O/s N.C.O's & men raided the Boche trench on our left. Enemy retaliated heavily with B+M, AMR, RRG, 9 mmRY 77mM. These spoilt until upon German co-operation work N.C.O.	See appendix B.2.

WAR DIARY or INTELLIGENCE SUMMARY

Army Form C. 2118.

Instructions regarding War Diaries and Intelligence Summaries are contained in F. S. Regs., Part II. and the Staff Manual respectively. Title pages will be prepared in manuscript.

(Erase heading not required.)

Hour, Date, Place		Summary of Events and Information	Remarks and references to Appendices
9.6.17.	CAMBRIN, R/S	Quiet all day in the line - B" H.Q. Outpost 65 & 63 kg 33 bays at Hper trench fire. Casualties 2/Lt Brotan & 1 oy & res OR. 3 wounded.	9.6.17. See appendix B.2.
10.6.17.	CAMBRIN, R/S	Situation normal - 8.30pm the artillery rather lift, with barrage for wire-cutting 10.15 - Weather fine - Casualties OR nil	10.6.17.
11.6.17 - 17.6.17	Support	Owing to the heavy hining place no men left at night, the whole Battery wise in the trench during the day. Weather miserable. Relieved by the 2/7 Warwickshire Regt. "A" Coy Bruker Hump - "B" Coy lift Cap St 3 "C" Coy village line - "D" Coy left barren line. Marched from Lef Carriestown Caviers when the coy for 2/5 Infr Regt - OR 3 killed - 3 wounded	11.6.17 - 17.6.17 See appendix A.6.i. See appendix B.2.
17.6.17.	CAMBRIN, R/S	Relieved by 2/7 Warwickshire Regt. Situation quiet. Casualties nil.	17.6.17. See appendix
18.6.17.	CAMBRIN, R/S	Situation normal - trench fire - Casualties 2/Lt J.P. Burne - Wounded - O.R. 2 killed 2/8	18.6.17.
19.6.17.	CAMBRIN, R/S	Situation normal - trench fire - Casualties R/S	19.6.17.
20.6.17	CAMBRIN, R/S	Situation quiet - trench dormy - Casualties R/S 2/Lt Shilman killed OR nil	20.6.17

WAR DIARY
or
INTELLIGENCE SUMMARY

Army Form C. 2118.

(Erase heading not required.)

Hour, Date, Place	Summary of Events and Information	Remarks and references to Appendices
20.6.17. CAMBRIN Right AM	Relieved by 1/K.R.R. Battalion - proceeded to BEUVRY - thence to La Pugnoy at 4.30 A.M. Weather fine - Casualties - nil.	See appendices A.2
22.6.17. La Pugnoy (Billets)	Ordinary Infantry Training	
26.6.17. La Pugnoy	Battalion less "D" Coy. left La Pugnoy at 10.45 a.m. entrained at Choques - at 3.33 pm arrived at town PLAGE Marched to St Pol. "D" Coy. entrained at 7.35 pm arrived at 11.30 pm At Long PLAGE Marched to St Pol	See appendices A.9
26.6.17 to 2.7.17	In Billets - Training Company leaving. Bathing in the Sea in the afternoon	

J. W. Bacquoy
Lt. Col
Coy 2/8 Br Manchester Regt

2/7/17.

Appendix A.
(Operation Orders)

SECRET.

2/8th Batt. MANCHESTER REGIMENT ORDER No.16.

Copy No..........
1/6/17.

1. "B" and "C" Companies 2/8th MANCH. R. will relieve xxx "C" and "D" Companies, 2/5th MANCH. R. in CAMBRIN LEFT on night of June 1st/2nd 1917.

2. A guide from 2/5th MANCH. R. will meet the head of Relief Companies at the junction of MUNSTER PARADE and RAILWAY ALLEY at 10 p.m.

3. Receipts will be given for all trench stores, etc. taken over.

4. Completion of relief will be reported by B.A.B.Code.

(Signed) G.McDougall, Capt. & Adjt.
2/8th Batt. Manchester Regt.

Issued at 8-30 p.m.

Copy No. 1.   Retained.
"   " 2.   199th Inf. Bgde.
"   " 3.   2/5th MANCH. R.
"   " 4.   O.C. "B" Coy. 2/8th MANCH. R.
"   " 5.   O.C. "C" Coy. 2/8th MANCH. R.
"   " 6/7. War Diary.

SECRET

2/8th Batt. MANCHESTER REGT. Order No.17.

Copy No..6......
3/6/17.

1. "D" Coy. will relieve "C" Coy. in CAMBRIN LEFT on June 3rd 1917.

2. Guide will meet the relieving Coy. at junction of QUARRY ALLEY and CUT into RAILWAY ALLEY at 9 a.m. on June 3rd.

3. "C" Coy. will move into hutments vacated by "D" Coy. at NOYELLES.

4. Receipts will be given for all trench stores, etc. taken over.

5. Completion of relief to be reported by B.A.B.Code.

(Signed) G.McDougall, Capt. & Adjt.
2/8th Batt. Manchester Regt.

Issued at 7-30 a.m.

Copy No.1......Retained.
 "   " 2......199th Inf.Bde.
 "   " 3......O.C. "C" Coy.
 "   " 4......O.C."D" Coy.
 "   " 5......T.O. & Q.M.
 "   " 6/7....War Diary.

SECRET.

2/8th BATT. MANCHESTER REGT. ORDER NO.12.

Copy No.1..
3/6/17.

1. Detachment XI Corps Cavalry Regt. will relieve "B" Coy. 2/8th MANCH. R. in CAMBRIN LEFT SUBSECTOR on June 4th 1917.
   "B" Coy. 2/8th MANCH. R. will move into NOYELLES.

2. Platoon Guides of "B" Coy. 2/8th MANCH. R. will meet relieving detachment at Junction of QUARRY ALLEY and CUT into RAILWAY ALLEY at 9 a.m. June 4th. Relieving Detachment will be led to this point by guides of 2/8th MANCH R. who will be at NOYELLES CROSS ROADS L.11.c.9.1. at 8-30 a.m.

3. Movement will be by platoons (not exceeding 40 O.R.) at 300 yards distance.

4. Receipts will be given for all trench stores, etc. taken over.

5. Completion of relief to be reported by B.A.B. Code to O.C. 2/6th MANCH. R. and O.C. 2/8th MANCH. R.

6. ACKNOWLEDGE.

Issued at 2-30 a.m.   (Signed) G.McDougall,Capt.& Adjt.
Copy No.1....Retained.   2/8th Batt.Manchester Regt.
  "   " 2....127th Inf.Bgde
  "   " 3....O.C.2/8th MANCH.R.
  "   " 4....O.C.Detachment,XI Corps.Cavalry.
  "   " 5....O.C."B" Coy.
  "   " 6....T.O.& Q.M.
  "   " 7....R.S.M.
  "   " 8/9...War Diary.

Appendix A.4

SECRET.

2/8th Batt. MANCHESTER REGIMENT ORDER No.13.

Copy No............
3/6/17.

1. One Company 2/8th MANCH. R. will relieve "D" Coy. 2/8th MANCH. R. (No.2 Coy.) in CAMBRIN LEFT SUBSECTOR on June 5th 1917.

   "D" Coy. 2/8th MANCH. R. will move into NOYELLES.

2. Relieving Coy. will leave VILLAGE LINE at 4 a.m. and proceed via RAILWAY ALLEY.

   Relieved Coy. will leave the trenches via GUT into QUARRY ALLEY and QUARRY ALLEY.

3. Receipts will be given for all trench stores, etc. taken over.

4. Completion of relief will be reported to O.C. 2/5th, 2/6th and 2/8th MANCH. R.

5. Acknowledge.

(Signed) G. McDougall, Capt. & Adjt
2/8th Batt. Manchester Regt.

Issued at 3-30 pm.

Copy No. 1. Retained.
  "   " 2. 199th Inf. Bde.
  "   " 3. O.C. 2/5th MANCH. R.
  "   " 4. O.C. 2/6th MANCH. R.
  "   " 5. O.C. "D" Coy. 2/8th MANCH. R.
  "   " 6. T.O. & Q.M.
  "   " 7. R.S.M.
  "   " 8/9 War Diary.

SECRET.   Opt A

2/8th BN. MANCHESTER REGIMENT ORDER NO. 30.

Copy No.....
4/8/17.

1. The Battalion will relieve the 2/7th MANCH. R. in CAMBRIN RIGHT Subsector to-morrow.

2. Route and Time Table attached.

3. Receipts will be given for all Trench Stores, Maps, Documents, etc. taken over, and copies forwarded to the Adjutant by 9 a.m. on 6/8/17.

4. All huts, billets, cookhouses, latrines, etc. are to be left clean.

5. Completion of relief to be reported by B.A.B. Code.

6. Acknowledge.

(Signed) C. McDougall, Capt. & Adjt.
2/8th Batt. Manchester Regt.

Issued at 6-30 p.m.

Copy No. 1.   Retained.
"   "   2.   199th Inf. Bde.
"   "   3.   2/8th MANCH. R.
"   "   4.   2/6th   do.
"   "   5.   2/7th   do.
"   "   6.   O.C. "A" Coy.
"   "   7.   "   "B" "
"   "   8.   "   "C" "
"   "   9.   "   "D" "
"   " 10.   "   "HQ" "
"   " 11.   T.O. & Q.M.
"   " 12.   R.S.M.
"   " 13.   M.O.
"   " 14/15.   War Diary.

Time & Route Table for Relief.

2/8/17

Relief of.	Coy.	by	Coy.	Time of leaving BOUZELLES.	Route.
RIGHT FIRING LINE.	"C" Coy. 2/7th M.R.		"A" Coy. 2/6th M.R.	8 p.m.	GORDON ALLEY SMITH ALLEY SAVILLE ROW.
CENTRE FIRING LINE.	"A" Coy. do.		"C" Coy. do.	8-30 p.m.	GORDON ALLEY DAVID ALLEY LEFT BOYAU.
LEFT FIRING LINE.	"D" Coy. do.		"B" Coy. do.	8 p.m.	GUARDS ALLEY.
RIGHT SUPPORT.	"B" Coy. do.		"D" Coy. do.	9 p.m.	GORDON ALLEY. DAVID ALLEY.

SECRET. Appendix A.6   Copy No 15

2/8th Bn. Manchester Regt. Order No. 21.

                                                    June 10th 1917.

1. The Battalion will be relieved by 2/7th Manchester Regt to-morrow, June 11th 1917.

2. Relief will begin at 5 a.m. and be complete by 10 a.m.

3. On being relieved the Battalion will go into BRIGADE SUPPORT and VILLAGE LINE as follows:-

    "A" Coy.   RAILWAY RESERVE TRENCH and CENTRAL KEEP (less 1 Platoon in RESERVE TRENCH)

    "B" Coy.   TOURBIERES REDOUBT via QUARRY ALLEY and VILLAGE LINE.

    "C" Coy.   RIGHT VILLAGE LINE, via LEFT BOYAU and QUARRY ALLEY.

    "D" Coy.   LEFT RESERVE TRENCH.

4. Where movement in the open is necessary, Officers or N.C.Os in charge of parties or Platoons must be careful to avoid being seen by the enemy. Should hostile aeroplanes appear, parties must leave the road and lie down.

5. Receipts will be taken for all trench stores, maps, documents etc handed over.

6. All trenches, dugouts, cookhouses and latrines must be left CLEAN.

7. Completion of relief to be reported by B.A.B. Code.

8. Acknowledge.

                                    (Sgd) G.McDougall, Captn
                                    Adjt. 2/8th Bn. Manchester Regt.

Issued at 7 p.m.

Copy No 1 Retained.
  "   " 2 199th Inf: Brigade.
  "   " 3 O.C. 2/8th Manch R.
  "   " 4 O.C. 2/5th   "
  "   " 5 O.C. 2/7th   "
  "   " 6 O.C. XX Corps Cavalry Detchment.
  "   " 7 O.C. A Coy.
  "   " 8 O.C. B Coy.
  "   " 9 O.C. C Coy.
  "   " 10 O.C. D Coy.
  "   " 11 O.C. H.Q. Coy.
  "   " 12 T.O. & Q.M.
  "   " 13 M.O.
  "   " 14 R.S.M.
  "   " 15/16 War Diary.

SECRET.   Copy No. 14

2/8th Bn. Manchester Regiment Order No. 22

June 16th 1917.

1. The Battalion will relieve 2/7th Manchester Regt in CAMBRIN RIGHT subsector to-morrow.

2. Time and Route Table attached.

3. Parties moving in relief must not be larger than Platoons and a minimum distance of 300 yards must be kept between parties. Should hostile aeroplanes appear when troops are moving in the open, troops must leave the road and lie down.

4. Receipts will be given for all Maps, Documents and trench stores taken over and copies forwarded to H.Q. by 9 a.m. June 18th. Emergency stores to be shown seperately.

5. All billets, trenches, cookhouses, latrines &c are to be left scrupulously clean.

6. Completion of relief to be immediately reported to H.Q. by B.A.B. Code.

7. Acknowledge.

(Signed) G. McDougall, Capt.
Adjt: 2/8th Bn. Manchester Regt.

Issued at 6-30 pm

Copy No.	1	Retained.
" "	2	199th Inf: Bde.
" "	3	2/5th Manor. R.
" "	4	2/6th " "
" "	5	2/7th " "
" "	6	"A" Coy.
" "	7	"B" "
" "	8	"C" "
" "	9	"D" "
" "	10	H.Q. "
" "	11	T.O. & Q.M.
" "	12	M.O.
" "	13	R.S.M.
" "	14/15	War Diary.

RELIEF TABLE

June 17th 1917.

Relief of.	Coy.	by	Coy.	Starting Time	Route.
Right Firing Line	"D" Coy 2/7th		"D" Coy 2/6th	4-0p.m.	RESERVE TRENCH SAVILLE ROW.
Centre Firing Line.	"B" Coy 2/7th		"C" Coy 2/6th	3-45 p.m.	QUARRY ALLEY LEFT BOYAU.
Left Firing Line	"A" Coy 2/7th		"B" Coy 2/6th	3-30p.m.	QUARRY ALLEY.
Right Support.	"C" Coy 2/7th		"A" Coy 2/6th	4-30p.m.	BART'S ALLEY.

Notes :- Each Coy will leave behind 1 officer to hand over to the Relieving Coy of 2/7th Manch Regt.

H.Q. Coy will start at 4-0p.m. and proceed via QUARRY ALLEY.

SECRET.   Appendix A 8   Copy No. 16

2/8th Bn. Manchester Regiment Order No. 23.

Refer: Bethune (Combined
Sheet) 1/40,000.   June 21st 1917.

1. The Battalion will be relieved by 1/K.R.R.C. today and move back into billets.

2. 3 Guides per Coy, 1 for H.Q. and 1 R.A.M.C. will meet the relieving Battalion at NOYELLES X Roads L 11 c 9 2 at 5 p.m.

3. Relieving Coys will leave NOYELLES in the following order and be led by the following routes:-

    1. Centre Coy.   CLARK'S KEEP – WINDY CORNER,
                      QUARRY ALLEY – LEFT BOYAU.

    2. Right Coy.   CLARK'S KEEP – GORDON ALLEY,
                      BART'S ALLEY – SAVILLE ROW.

    3. LEFT COY.   CLARK'S KEEP – WINDY CORNER
                      –QUARRY ALLEY.

    4. SUPPORT COY.   CLARK'S KEEP – GORDON ALLEY
                      BARTS ALLEY.

    5. H.Q.   CLARK'S KEEP – GORDON ALLEY.

4. Movement will be by sections at 100 yards distance.

5. From 7-30 p.m. QUARRY ALLEY in rear of Battn H.Q. will be an IN trench and GORDON ALLEY on OUT trench only.

6. On completion of relief Companies will march independently to billets at LAPUGNOY. March discipline is to be strictly observed.

7. All Defence Schemes, Secret Maps, Aeroplane Photos, Trench Stores etc, will be handed over to relieving Units and receipts obtained. A copy will be sent to Battalion H.Q. on arrival in billets. All 1/100000 – 1/80000 – 1/250000 maps now in possession of Units will **not** be handed over but kept.

8. Completion of relief will be reported at once by B.A.B. Code.

9. One Officer per Coy. will remain in the line until 12 noon on 22nd June when they rejoin the Battalion.

10. Acknowledge.

                                    (Sgd) G. McDougall, Capt & Adjt.
                                          2/8th Bn. Manchester Regiment.

Issued at 8 a.m.

Copy No 1   Retained.
"   " 2   199th Inf: Bde:
"   " 3   O.C. 1/K.R.R.C.
"   " 4   O.C. 2/5th MANCH R.
"   " 5   O.C. 2/6th MANCH R.
"   " 6   O.C. 2/7th MANCH R.
"   " 7   O.C. "A" Coy.
"   " 8   O.C. "B" "
"   " 9   O.C. "C" "
"   " 10   O.C. "D" "
"   " 11   O.C. H.Q. "
"   " 12   T.O.
"   " 13   M.O.
"   " 14   R.S.M.
"   " 15/16 War Diary.

SECRET.   Copy No. 16
                                                        June 24th 1917.

2/8th Bn. Manchester Regt. Order No. 24.

Reference Bethune Combined Sheet 1/40000.

1. The Battalion less "D" Coy. and 1 Travelling Kitchen will entrain at CHOQUES at 3-33 p.m. on 25th inst:

    "D" Coy with one Travelling Kitchen will entrain at CHOQUES at 7-33 p.m. on 25th inst.

    Destination XV Corps Training Area.

2. Transport less 1 Travelling Kitchen will leave the Transport Lines at 11 a.m. and march to CHOQUES Station (D 5 a 9 5)
   O.C. "A" Coy and O.C. "B" Coy will each detail a loading and unloading party of 3 N.C.O's and 30 men to march with the Transport.
   Transport personnel and loading parties will travel in carrages as near as possible to the trucks containing horses and vehicles.

3. The remainder of the Battalion less "D" Coy will march to CHOQUES Station in the following order.
                    H.Q.
                    "A" Coy.
                    "B" Coy.
                    "C" Coy.
   Starting point LAPUGNOY CHURCH (D 15 d 0 0)
   The head of the column will pass the starting point at 12-45 p.m.

4. "D" Coy's Travelling Kitchen will leave the Transport Lines at 3 p.m. 2nd Lt. COLLIS and 6 men of "D" Coy will march with the Travelling Kitchen.
   Remainder of "D" Coy will march from their billet at 4-30 p.m.

5. All Officer's Kits must be ready for loading outside their billets at 9 a.m.

6. The strictest discipline is to be maintained throughout the train journey. The most careful attention must be paid to all the points mentioned in para 4 of Battn Order d/d 23/6/17.

7. All billets are to be left scrupulously clean.

8. Acknowledge.

                                        (Sgd) G.McDougall Capt & Adjt
                                        2/8th Bn. Manchester Regiment.

Issued at 4 p.m.

    Copy No. 1   Retained.
       "   " 2   199th Inf: Bde.
       "   " 3   C.O.
       "   " 4   2nd in Command.
       "   " 5   O.C. "A" Coy.
       "   " 6   O.C. "B" "
       "   " 7   O.C. "C" "
       "   " 8   O.C. "D" "
       "   " 9   O.C. H.Q.Coy.
       "   " 10   T.O.
       "   " 11   M.O.
       "   " 12   Capt. R.H.King.
       "   " 13   2nd Lt. Collis.
       "   " 14   R.S.M.
       "   " 15)
       "   " 16)   War Diary.

Appendix "B"
(map)

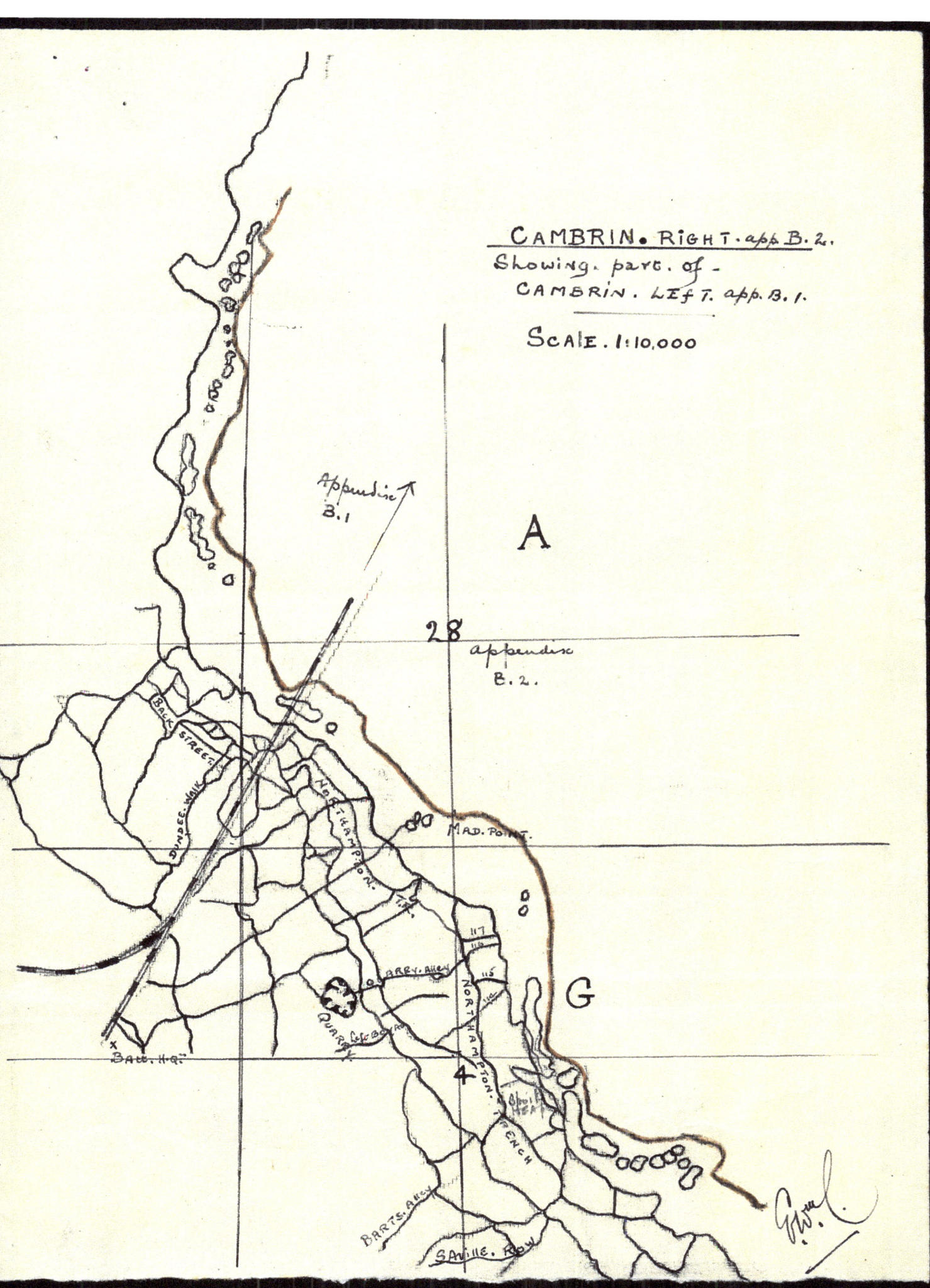

1915

CONFIDENTIAL

War Diary
of
2/8th Batt Manchester Regt.

From July 1st 1917. To July 31st 1917.

(Volume I)

WAR DIARY
or
INTELLIGENCE SUMMARY

(Erase heading not required.)

Army Form C. 2118.

Hour, Date, Place	Summary of Events and Information	Remarks and references to Appendices
2.7.17. ST. POL	Marched to Beach for training. Bathing in the afternoon	E.B.C.
6.7.17		
8.7.17		
9.7.17. COUDEKERQUE-BRANCH	Marched to Coudekerque Branch - arrived at billets 12.30 p.m.	E.W. See appendix A1.
10.7.17. COUDEKERQUE-BRANCH	100 O.R. per Coy. attached to R.E.'s - B/n. marched to Beach for training.	Ersl.
11.7.17. COUDEKERQUE-BRANCH	Batt: Marched to Moeres - Stand to all day.	E.W.
12.7.17. GHYVELDE	A & D Coys left Coude Kerque - Branch an motor lorries - Carried out A. Working parties for A.O.C. (morning Shells cs). B & C Coys marched to Ghyvelde - Bivouac Huttments.	Ersl. See Whernus A.2.
13.7.17. GHYVELDE	A & D Coys - Working parties for A.O.C. B & C Coys - Training	Ersl.
14.7.17. GHYVELDE	B & C Coys - Working parties for A.O.C. A & D Coys - Training	R. W. C.
15.7.17. OOST-DUNKERQUE-BAINS.	Batt. Moved by motor through BRAYDUNES - ADINKERQUE - LA-PANNE - COXYDE - COXYDE-BAINS - 6 OOST-DUNKERQUE-BAINS Billets in RINCH - CAMP.	Ersl. See appendix A.3.
16.7.17. OOST-DUNKERQUE-BAINS.	Rinch - Camp. Training.	Ersl.
17.7.17. OOST-DUNKERQUE-BAINS.	Rinch - Camp. Training.	Ersl.

Army Form C. 2118.

WAR DIARY
or
INTELLIGENCE SUMMARY
(Erase heading not required.)

Instructions regarding War Diaries and Intelligence
Summaries are contained in F.S. Regs., Part II.
and the Staff Manual respectively. Title pages
will be prepared in manuscript.

Hour, Date, Place	Summary of Events and Information	Remarks and references to Appendices
14.7.17. OOST. DUNKIRQUE - BAINS.	Rinch-camp - Training.	&c.
19.7.17 OOST DUNKIRQUE BAINS.	Rinch cap. Training.	&c.
20.7.17	Men from R.E.º returned to A.C. & D. Corps.	&c.
21.7.17 OOST DUNKIRQUE - BAINS.	Batt. marches to St. Idesbald - C & D Coys left coast. Cm. & D Defence. A + B training	&c. See appendix p.24
22.7.17 + 23.7.17		
24.7.17 OOST DUNKIRQUE BAINS. 25.7.17 26.7.17 27.7.17	B" moved to Camp to Relieve OOST- DUNKIRQUE - BAINS.	&c. See appendix A.5
28.7.17. COAST DEFENCE ST. IDESBALD	O. & D Coast Defence left hacker. A + B Training	&c. See appendix A.6
29.7.17. dito	Atts. Coy Commanders left follow - St. Heneric information own.	&c.

WAR DIARY
or
INTELLIGENCE SUMMARY.
(Erase heading not required.)

Army Form C. 2118.

Instructions regarding War Diaries and Intelligence Summaries are contained in F.S. Regs., Part II. and the Staff Manual respectively. Title pages will be prepared in manuscript.

Hour, Date, Place	Summary of Events and Information	Remarks and references to Appendices
30/7/17. OOST Dunkerque.	Bn moved to Camp Yorkshire	all. See Appendix A 7.
	Bn took over Right sub sector NIEUPORT BAINS sector on night 30/31/7/17.	all See Appendix A 8
31/7/17 Right subsector NIEUPORT BAINS sector.	Situation normal. Casualties Nil.	nil

J.R. Bagford
Lieut Colonel
Commg 9th Bn Manchester Regiment

Appendices
A1 to A8.   July 1917

(Operation Orders)

SECRET.

2/8th. Bn. Manchester Regt.   Copy No. 13

8. 7. 17.

Ref Map Sheet 19. 1/40.000.

1. The Battalion will move on 9th July to the S of DUNKERQUE-BERGUES Canal and billet in COUDEKERQUE BRANCHE.

2. The Battalion will march as per attached March table.

3. Two baggage waggons will report at Transport Lines at 7-0.a.m. on 9th July. Officers Kits must be dumped ready for loading outside Company messes at 7-30.a.m. Companies must have their L.G. Wagons loaded by 6-0.p.m. 8th July.

4. Billeting party will meet the Battalion at H 10 d 4. 1 and conduct Companies to their billeting areas.

5. All O.C. Companies will at one on arrival forward the location of the Company to Battalion Headquarters.

6. Billets, Transport lines, Store Rooms etc are to be left absolutely clean.

7. Unexpended portion of days Rations will be carried in the Cookers.
Refilling point for Supplies will be at COUDEKERQUE BRANCHE (H 11. c 5. 5.)

8. Acknowledge.

Issued at ..4 P.M...

Copy No 1. Retained.
"   "   2. H.Q. 199th Infantry Brigade.
"   "   3. C. O.
"   "   4. 2nd in Command.
"   "   5 O.C. "A" Coy.
"   "   6. O.C. "B" "
"   "   7. O.C. "C" "
"   "   8. O.C. "D" "
"   "   9 Transport Officer and Q.M.
"   "10 M. O.
"   "11 R.S.M.
"   "12/13 War Diary.

G McDougall Capt & Adjt.
2/8th . Bn. Manchester Regt.

MARCH TABLE.

2/8th Batt. Manchester Regt. – 12/7/17.

Order of March.	Starting Point.	Time of passing starting point.	Route.	Destination
H.Q.	Square in front of H.Q. Mess – H 16 b 6.8.	6-15 am.	)	
"A" Coy.	do.	5-15 am.	) Rd. junction) H.6.b.1.8.	) Camp
"C" Coy.	Canal Bridge, where canal, road and railway meet, close to "D" Coy. Officers' Mess H.12.c.0.0.	6-5 am.	) thence to) main FURNES) road to PONT) DE GHYVELDE) D.15.b. –) GHYVELDE.	) or) Billets) at) GHYVELDE.
"B" Coy.	do.	6-8 am.	)	
"D" Coy.	do.	6-11 am.	)	
Transport.	Q.M.Stores. H.10.d.5.1.	6-25 am.		

MARCH TABLE.

	Starting Point.	Times of passing starting point	Route.
H. Q.	Square in front of Church of St Pol	10-0.a.m.	DUNKERQUE- COUDEKERQUE BRANCHE.
"D" Coy	Do	10-1.a.m.	Do
"C" "	Do	10-5.a.m.	Do
"B"	Junction of Rue de la republique and Avenue Maurice Bertaux	10-15.a.m.	Do
"A"	Do	10-19.a.m.	Do
1st Line Transport.	Do	10-25.a.m.	Do.

There will be an interval of 200 yds between Companies and between "A" Coy and Transport.

G. McDougall Capt & Adjt.
2/8th .Manchester Regt

2/8th Batt. Manchester Regiment.

Secret.

OPERATION ORDER NO. 26.

Copy No....
12/7/17.

Ref. Map Sheet No. 1/40,000.

1. The Battalion will march to GHYVELDE to-day.

2. March Table attached. Intervals of 200 yards will be maintained between Companies, and between rear Company and Transport.

3. Particular attention is to be paid to march discipline, especially as regards dressing and keeping to the right of the road.

4. All billets, storerooms, transport lines, etc. are to be left perfectly clean.

5. Location of Company Headquarters and Transport Lines will be reported to Battalion Headquarters on arrival at destination.

6. Acknowledge.

(Signed) G.McDougall, Capt. & Adjt.
2/8th Batt.Manchester Regt.

Issued at 1-30 a.m.
Copy No.	
1	Retained.
2	199th Inf. Bgde.
3	C.O.
4	2nd in Command.
5	O.C. "A" Coy.
6	" " "B" Coy.
7	" " "C" Coy.
8	" " "D" Coy.
9	" " "H.Q." Coy.
10	M.O.
11	T.O.
12	R.S.M.
13	Chaplain.
14	War Diary.
15	do.

SECRET.

Appendix A 3

2/8th Batt. Manchester Regt.

OPERATION ORDER NO. 97.

Map Reference. Sheet 11 S.E. 1/20,000.

Copy No.....
15/7/17.

1. The Battalion will move to 1st Division Area OOST DUNKERKE - OOST DUNKERKE BAINS - COXYDE BAINS to-morrow, and will take over from 60th K.R.R.C. at BIRCH CAMP R.35.b.3.0.

2. The Battalion will parade in Camp ready to move at 8-30 a.m.

3. The route will be ADINKERKE - Road junction N.26.d.58.25 - KERKE PANNE - COXYDE - COXYDE BAINS.

4. All present billets, huts, etc. are to be left absolutely clean.

Issued at 3-30 a.m.

(Signed) G. McDougall, Capt. & Adjt
2/8th Bn. Manchester Regiment.

Copy No. 1 Retained.
" 2 199th Inf. Bde.
" 3 C.O.
" 4 2nd in Command.
" 5 O.C. "A" Coy.
" 6 " "B" "
" 7 " "C" "
" 8 " "D" "
" 9 " "H.Q." Coy.
" 10 T.O.
" 11 M.O.
" 12 R.S.M.
" 13/14 War Diary.

SECRET.

2/8th Bn. Manchester Regiment.

Order No.28.

20/7/17.

Copy No. ....

Refce. Sheet 11. 1/20,000.

1. The Battalion will relieve 2/7th Bn. Manchester R. in Left.Sub-Sector, Coast Defence, tomorrow, 21/7/17.

2. One guide per Coy. of 2/7th MANCH. R. will be at Cross Roads W.6.a.9.6. at 9-45 a.m.

3. The Battalion will march from Camp in the following order at 9 a.m.
    "D" Coy.   relieving "B" Coy. 2/7th.
    "B" "   "   "D" "   "
    "C" "   "   "A" "   "
    "A" "   "   "C" "   "
    "HQ" "

4. Lewis Gun Wagons and Cookers will march immediately in rear of their respective Coys. On arrival at destination, Lewis Gun Wagons must be immediately unloaded, and returned to Camp.
Officers' Baggage must be dumped ready for loading between Orderly Room and the Road by 8-30 a.m.
The Transport Officer will arrange to move Q.M.Stores etc. in the course of the day.

5. An Advance party of 2/7th LAN. FUS. will arrive at 8 a.m. to take over the Camp.

6. All huts, cookhouses, etc. will be left absolutely clean.

7. Receipts will be given for all trench stores, maps, etc. taken over, and a copy forwarded to Battalion Headquarters by 6 p.m.

8. Completion of relief will be immediately reported to Batt.H.Q.

9. Acknowledge.

(Signed) G. McDougall, Capt. & Adjt.
2/8th Batt. Manchester Regiment.

Issued at 8 p.m.
Copy No.1.   Retained.
      2.   199th Inf.Bde.
      3.   2/7th MANCH. R.
      4.   2/7th LAN.Fus.
      5.   C.O.
      6.   2nd in Command.
      7.   O.C. "A" Coy.
      8.   "   "B" "
      9.   "   "C" "
     10.   "   "D" "
     11.   "   "HQ" "
     12.   M.O.
     13.   T.O.
   14&15. R.S.M.
     16/16 War Diary.

SECRET.

2/8th Battalion Manchester Regiment.

ORDER NO. 29.   Copy N ....
                   24/7/17.

Reference Sheet 11, S.E. 1/20,000

1. The Battalion will be relieved by the 2/9th MANCH. R. in Left Sector, Coast Defence to-day, July 24th, and will move to CAMP LEFEVRE.

2. Companies will be relieved as under :-

   "A" Coy. by "A" Coy. 2/9th MANCH. R.
   "B" "   " "B" "   "   "   "
   "C" "   " "C" "   "   "   "
   "D" "   " "D" "   "   "   "

3. Relief will begin at 2-30 p.m.

4. Companies will hand over Billets, Trench Stores, Maps, etc. to relieving Companies. Receipts will be taken and copies sent in to Battalion H.Q. by 9 a.m. to-morrow, July 25th.

5. On completion of Relief, Companies will march independently to CAMP LEFEVRE, R.32.b, and take over quarters vacated by the corresponding Coys. of 2/7th MANCH. R.

6. Lewis Gun Limbers will be placed by the Transport Officer outside Coy. H.Q. at 2-30 p.m. and must be immediately loaded. Companies will detail parties to accompany the limbers, immediately off-load them on arrival at Camp and guard the guns and stores till arrival of the Company. Travelling Kitchens must be ready for removal at 2-30 p.m.

7. All billets, cookhouses, latrines, etc. must be left absolutely clean.

8. Completion of relief will be immediately reported to new Batt. H.Q. at R.32.b.8.8. (CAMP LEFEVRE).

9. Acknowledge.

                    (Signed) G. McDougall, Captain & Adjt.
                             2/8th Battalion Manchester Regiment.

Issued at 1 p.m.
Copy No. 1.- Retained.
 "   2   199th Inf. Bde.
 "   3   198th "   "
 "   4   2/9th MANCH. R.
 "   5   O.C. "A" Coy.
 "   6   "   "B" "
 "   7   "   "C" "
 "   8   "   "D" "
 "   9   "   "H.Q." "
 "   10   Transport Officer.
 "   11   Medical Officer.
 "   12   Chaplain.
 "   13/14   War Diary.

SECRET.

2/8th Batt. Manchester Regiment.

Operation Order No. 30.

Copy No. 14
27/7/17.

1. The Battalion will relieve 2/9th MANCH. R. in Left Sector, COAST DEFENCE, to-morrow.

2. Disposition will be as follows :-

    Front Line.   Right Coy. "C" Coy.
                  Left   "   "D" "

    Support.   Right Coy. "A" "
                  Left   "   "B" "

3. Companies will march independently from Camp as under :-

    "D" Coy. at 9-15 a.m.
    "C" "   " 9-30 a.m.
    "A" "   " 9-45 a.m.
    "B" "   " 10 a.m.
    "HQ" "   " 10 a.m.

4. Transport Lines will be exchanged with 2/9th MANCH. R.

5. Lewis Gun Wagons and Cookers will march independently immediately in rear of their own Coys.
On arrival at destination Lewis Gun Wagons must be immediately unloaded and returned to Camp.
Officers baggage must be dumped ready for loading outside Q.M. Stores at 9-30 a.m.

6. All huts, cookhouses, etc. will be left absolutely clean.

7. Receipts will be given for all trench stores, maps, etc. taken over, and a copy forwarded to Batt. H.Q. by 6 pm.

8. Completion of relief will be immediately reported to Batt. H.Q.

9. Acknowledge.

(Sgd) G. McDougall, Capt. & Adjt.
2/8th Batt. Manchester Regiment.

Issued at 10 pm.
Copy No. 1. Retained.   Copy No. 8.   O.C. "C" Coy.
 "   " 2. 198th Inf. Bgd.   "   " 9.   "   "D" "
 "   " 3. 2/9th MANCH. R.   "   " 10.   "   "HQ" "
 "   " 4. C.O.   "   " 11.   M.O.
 "   " 5. 2nd in Command.   "   " 12.   T.O.
 "   " 6. O.C. "A" Coy.   "   " 13.   R.S.M.
 "   " 7. "   "B" "   "   " 14/15. War Diary.

SECRET

2/8th Batt. Manchester Regiment Order No. 31.

Copy No..........
30/7/17.

Reference Sheet 11, S.E. 1/20,000

1. The Battalion will be relieved by the 2/6th LAN. FUS. in Left Subsector, Coast Defence, today, July 30th, and will move to CAMP JUNIAC. (X.3.a.)

2. Relief will begin at 10 a.m.

3. Companies will hand over Billets, Trench Stores, Work Reports, etc. to relieving Companies. Receipts will be taken and copies sent in to Battalion H.Q. by 6 p.m. to-day.

4. On completion of relief, Companies will march independently to CAMP JUNIAC (X.3.a.), and take up quarters vacated by corresponding Coys. of 2/6th LAN. FUS.

5. Lewis Gun Limbers will be placed by the Transport Officer outside Coy.H.Q. at 10 a.m., and must be immediately loaded. Coys. will detail parties to accompany the limbers, and immediately offload them on arrival at Camp. Travelling Kitchens must be ready for removal at 10 a.m.

6. All billets, cookhouses, latrines, etc. must be left absolutely clean.

7. Completion of relief will be immediately reported to Batt.HQ Completion of move will be immediately reported to new Batt.H.Q. at CAMP JUNIAC (X.3.a.).

8. Acknowledge.

(Sgd) G.McDougall, Capt. & Adjt.
2/8th Batt. Manchester Regiment

Issued at 9 a.m.
Copy No. 1. Retained.
" " 2. 198th Inf.Bde.
" " 3. 2/6th LAN. Fus.
" " 4. C.O.
" " 5. 2nd in Command.
" " 6. O.C. "A" Coy.
" " 7. " "B" "
" " 8. " "C" "
" " 9. " "D" "
" " 10. " "HQ" "
" " 11. T.O.
" " 12. M.O.
" " 13. Chaplain.
" " 14. R.S.M.
" " 15/16. War Diary.

SECRET.   Annex.. A 8
         2/5th Bn. Manchester Regt. Order No. ...

Refce. Sheet :-   Copy No. ..14.....
Belgium .... 1/..,000.   30/7/17.

1. The Battalion will relieve 2/6th LAN. Fus. in
   FIRST POSITION, MIDDLE POINT SECTOR, on
   night of 30/31st July 1917.

2. ...ing our platoon from 2/6th LAN. FUS. will
   .... old H.Q.....? by 9-30 p.m. July 30th/17

3. Disposition in the Line will be as follows :-
         1st Coy.   "A" Coy.
         2nd Coy.   "B" "
         3rd Coy.   "C" "
         4th Coy.   "D" "

4. Coys. will march from camp quoted in above
   order. Leading platoon of "A" Coy. will march
   at 7.30 p.m. 150 yds. distance will be
   maintained between platoons.

5. Coys. will go into the Line in strength not
   exceeding 105 O.R. Details will be left in
   Camp under 2/Lieut. ASHTON.

6. All maps, aeroplane photos, diagrams schemes,
   tr.nch diagrams, S.A.A., etc. will be taken
   over and duplicate receipt sent to Orderly Room
   by 12 noon the day following relief.

7. Completion of Relief will be reported to Batt.
   H.Q. by runner, using the word "MANCHESTER".

                    (Signed) C. McDougall, Capt. & Adjt.
                        2/5th Battalion Manchester Regt.

Issued at 10 a.m.

Copy No. 1. Retained.
"   " 2. ists Inf. Bde.
"   " 3. 5/8th LAN. FUS.
"   " 4. O.C.
"   " 5. 2nd in Command.
"   " 6. O.C. "A" Coy.
"   " 7.   "   "B" "
"   " 8.   "   "C" "
"   " 9.   "   "D" "
"   " 10.   "   W.O.P.D. & details.
"   " 11. H.Q. XXXXXXX
"   " 12. R.O.
"   " 13. R.S.M.
"   " 14,15. War Diary.

Vol 6

CONFIDENTIAL.

WAR DIARY

of

2/8th Batt. Manchester Regiment.

From August 1st 1917.   To August 31st 1917.

Volume 1.

ARM
2-9-17

Army Form C. 2118.

WAR DIARY
or
INTELLIGENCE SUMMARY.
(Erase heading not required.)

Instructions regarding War Diaries and Intelligence Summaries are contained in F. S. Regs., Part II. and the Staff Manual respectively. Title pages will be prepared in manuscript.

Date	Hour, Date, Place	Summary of Events and Information	Remarks and references to Appendices
1-8-17	NIEUPORT BAINS SECTOR (Right sub-sector)	"A" Coy - Right firing line, "C" Coy - Left firing line, "B" Coy - Support "D" Coy - Reserve. Weather fine - Casualties nil.	Gist
2-8-17	R.S.S.	Patrol of 3 men swam YSER & reached enemy 2nd line returning safely Weather wet. Casualties 1 O.R. killed. 4 O.R. wounded.	Gist
3-8-17	R.S.S.	Weather wet - Casualties 1 O.R. wounded, 1 O.R. gassed	Gist
4-8-17	R.S.S.	Handed over B. Coy front to H.Q.H. Bomb and A. Coy relieved B. Coy of 2/5 Manchester Regt. Casualties 3 O.R. killed, 1 O.R. wounded (on duty) weather wet	Gist
5-8-17	R.S.S.	Weather wet - Casualties, 1 O.R. killed, 10 O.R. wounded, 1 O.R. wounded (on duty)	Gist
6-8-17	R.S.S.	Weather fine - Casualties 3 O.R. wounded including 2 on duty.	Gist
7-8-17	R.S.S.	Weather fine - Casualties nil	Gist
8-8-17	R.S.S.	Weather fine - Casualties 3 O.R. wounded	Gist
9-8-17	R.S.S.	Weather fine - Casualties nil	Gist
10-8-17	R.S.S.	Weather fine - Casualties 3 O.R. wounded	Gist
11-8-17	R.S.S.	Night 11/12th. Bn relieved by 2/7 & 2/8 Manchester Regts. relief complete 2-30am (Trenches vacated by 2/7 Manchester Regt. taken over by 2nd YORKSHIRE Regt.)	Gist (see appendix A.1.)
12-8-17	Camp - YORKSHIRE (Terries)	Weather fine - Casualties 1 O.R. killed, 3 O.R. wounded - including last day Working parties for R.E.s & Australian Tunnelling Coy. weather fine Casualties, 1 O.R. wounded	Gist
13-8-17	do	Working parties - weather fine. Casualties nil	Gist
14-8-17	do	Working parties - weather fine - Casualties nil	Gist
15-8-17	do	Working parties - "C" Coy NIEUPORT BAINS - on working party - Casualties 1 O.R. wounded at duty - weather fine	Gist

Army Form C. 2118.

WAR DIARY
or
INTELLIGENCE SUMMARY.
(Erase heading not required.)

Date	Hour, Date, Place	Summary of Events and Information	Remarks and references to Appendices
20.8.17	CAMP YORKSHIRE (Ivoire)	Working parties to 3. Co. 8 Tunnelling Coy - Casualties 2 O.R. wounded (1 at duty)	Cloze (APPENDIX A(c)).
21.8.17	do	Smith sector by gassed. B[tn] marched to camp WILTSHIRE - relief complete 5 pm. Casualties nil - weather fine	Cloze
22.8.17	CAMP WILTSHIRE	night of 21/22 "B" Coy attached to Barrin - casualties nil. weather fine	Cloze
23.8.17	do	Working parties for Tunnelling Coy - weather fine - casualties nil	Cloze
24.8.17	do	do - casualties 7 O.R. wounded (incl. 1 at duty)	Cloze
25.8.17	do	do - casualties nil - weather fine	Cloze
26.8.17	do	do - casualties - weather fine	Cloze
27.8.17	do	do - casualties nil - weather fine	Cloze
28.8.17	do	do - casualties 1 O.R. killed, 1 O.R. wounded	Cloze
29.8.17	do	Coop stilled during afternoon - casualties 1 O.R. killed, 2 O.R. wounded (at duty). 6 4" & 8" Coy attached Australian Tunnelling Coy	Cloze
30.8.17	do	Coop stilled during afternoon - casualties 3 O.R. wounded, 2 O.R. wounded (at duty) - "C" Coy attached to Australian Tunnelling Coy. Working parties - casualties nil	Cloze
31.8.17	do	Working parties - Casualties nil	Cloze

J.P. Dockson Lt Col.
Cmdg 96 Manchester Regt

APPENDICES A(1) & A(2)

Appendix
A.14

SECRET.

2/8th Battalion Manchester Regiment.

Order No. 33.

Copy No. 14
11/8/17.

Ref. GOXXD2 1/20,000
SECRET TRENCH MAP NO. 5.
(LOMBAERTZYDE)

1. The Battalion will be relieved by 2/7th MANCH. R. on night of 11/12th August 1917.

2. Companies will detail 1 guide per platoon to meet relieving Battalion at N 26 d 0.4. at 8-30 p.m. Guides will assemble at Bn. H.Q. at 6-30 p.m.

3. On relief the Battalion will move into CAMP YORKSHIRE (JUNIAC), vacated by 2/7th MANCH. R.

4. Movement E. of OOST DUNKERQUE - OOST DUNKERQUE BAINS ROAD to be by platoons at 200 yards interval. O.s.C. Companies may use their discretion in movening by sections if they wish to do so.

5. All trench stores, maps, details of work, progress, etc. will be handed over. Copies of receipts will be forwarded to Bn. H.Q. by 8 a.m. on Aug. 12th.

6. Completion of relief to be immediately reported to Bn. H.Q. by Code word "JAM".

7. Acknowledge.

(Signed) G. McDougall, Capt. & Adjt.
2/8th Batt. Manchester Regt.

Issued at 8 a.m.

Copy No. 1.	198th Inf. Bde.
" " 2.	2/7th MANCH. R.
" " 3.	C.O.
" " 4.	2nd in Command.
" " 5.	O.C "A" Coy.
" " 6.	" "B" "
" " 7.	" "C" "
" " 8.	" "D" "
" " 9.	" Details.
" "10.	M.O.
" "11.	T.O. & Q.M.
" "12.	R.S.M.
" "13/14.	War Diary.
" "15.	Retained.

Appendix A(2)

SECRET.

2/8th Batt. Manchester Regiment.

Order No. 34.   Copy No. 14
                  19/8/17.

Reference COXYDE 1/20,000.

1. The Battalion will be relieved by 2/8th Bn. Lancashire Fusiliers to-morrow, Aug. 20th 1917.

2. Relief will begin at 3 pm. and will be completed by 7 pm.

3. On relief the Battalion will move into WILTSHIRE CAMP vacated by 2/8th Bn. Lancashire Fusiliers. Companies will proceed independently to WILTSHIRE CAMP by shortest route. A minimum distance of 200 yards will be kept between platoons.

4. The Transport Officer and the Quartermaster will arrange for removal of Q.M. Stores throughout the day.

5. Officers' Baggage will be dumped at the Camp entrance (clear of the sand) by 9 a.m.

6. All huts, cookhouses, latrines, etc. are to be left clean.

7. The working party found by "C" Coy. will be taken over by 2/8th Bn. Lancashire Fusiliers from night of 21/22nd August inclusive.

8. Completion of relief in YORKSHIRE CAMP will be reported to Bn. H.Q. YORKSHIRE CAMP by code word "BASG", and completion of move to Bn. H.Q. in WILTSHIRE CAMP by code word "BUST".

9. Acknowledge.

(Sgd) G. McDougall, Capt. & Adjt.
2/8th Bn. Manchester Regiment.

Issued at 6 pm.

Copy No. 1.   108th Inf. Bde.
"   " 2.   2/8th Bn. Lancashire Fusiliers.
"   " 3.   C.O.
"   " 4.   2nd in Command.
"   " 5.   O.C. "A" Coy.
"   " 6.   " "B" "
"   " 7.   " "C" "
"   " 8.   " "D" "
"   " 9.   " "HQ" "
"   "10.   M.O.
"   "11.   T.O. & Q.M.
"   "12.   R.S.M.
"   "13/14. War Diary.
"   "15. Retained.

CONFIDENTIAL.

WAR DIARY
of
2/8th Batt. Manchester Regt.
from
1st Sept. - 30th Sept. 1917.

VOLUME VII.

Appendix.

1. Operation Orders.

Army Form C. 2118.

WAR DIARY
or
INTELLIGENCE SUMMARY.
(Erase heading not required.)

Instructions regarding War Diaries and Intelligence Summaries are contained in F.S. Regs., Part II. and the Staff Manual respectively. Title pages will be prepared in manuscript.

Hour, Date, Place	Summary of Events and Information	Remarks and references to Appendices
1.9.17 WILTSHIRE CAMP COXYDE BAINS	Battalion furnished working parties and carried on ordinary training Casualties - Nil.	
2.9.17 WILTSHIRE CAMP	Working parties and Training Casualties - Nil	
3.9.17 WILTSHIRE CAMP	Working parties and Training Casualties Nil	
4.9.17 WILTSHIRE CAMP	Working parties and Training Casualties - Nil	
5.9.17 ST IDESBALD CARDIFF CAMP	Battalion under orders moved camp to Cardiff Camp. St Idesbald by ½ Bn & ½ Bn. Reconnoitred new lines. Casualties Nil	See Operation Order No 35
6.9.17 ST IDESBALD	Battalion Training - Casualties Nil	
7.9.17 ST IDESBALD	Battalion Training - Casualties - Nil	
8.9.17 ST IDESBALD	Battalion Training - Casualties - Nil	
9.9.17 ST IDESBALD	Battalion Training - Casualties Nil	
10.9.17 ST IDESBALD	Battalion Training. Weather fine. Casualties - Nil	
11.9.17 ST IDESBALD	Battalion Training "Cath. fine" Casualties - Nil	
12.9.17 ST IDESBALD	Battalion Training. Weather fine Casualties 2 OR (2nd duty)	
13.9.17 ST IDESBALD	Battalion Training. Weather fine "A" Coy attached R.E. Training Coy Casualties nil	
14.9.17 ST IDESBALD	Battalion Scheme W of La PANNE Casualties 2/Lt R Groves slightly wounded	
15.9.17 ST IDESBALD	Battalion Scheme W of LA PANNE Casualties Nil	

Army Form C. 2118.

WAR DIARY
or
INTELLIGENCE SUMMARY.
(Erase heading not required.)

Instructions regarding War Diaries and Intelligence Summaries are contained in F.S. Regs., Part II. and the Staff Manual respectively. Title pages will be prepared in manuscript.

Hour, Date, Place	Summary of Events and Information	Remarks and references to Appendices
16.9.17 ST IDESBALD CARDIFF CAMP	Church Parade. Weather fine. Casualties – nil	
17.9.17 ST IDESBALD	Brigade Scheme W. of LA PANNE. Weather fine. Casualties – nil	
18.9.17 ST IDESBALD	Brigade Bombing Competition. Weather fine in morning & showery. Casualties – nil	
19.9.17 ST IDESBALD	Relieved 2/4 East Lancashire Regt. in Right Sub Sector, NIEUPORT BAINS SECTOR. "C" Coy Right Firing Line. "B" Coy Left Firing Line. "D" Coy Close Support. 1 platoon "D" Coy in Close Support Reserve. Casualties – nil. Details moved to COXYDE BAINS	See Operation Orders No. 26
20.9.17 R.S.S. NIEUPORT BAINS	1 Platoon "D" Coy was relieved by Details and returned to Close Support. Weather fine. Casualties – nil.	
21.9.17 R.S.S. NIEUPORT BAINS	Situation normal. Weather fine. Casualties – nil	
22.9.17 R.S.S. NIEUPORT BAINS	Situation normal. Weather fine. Casualties – nil	
23.9.17 R.S.S. NIEUPORT BAINS	Situation normal. Weather fine. Casualties for command.	
24.9.17 R.S.S. NIEUPORT BAINS	Relieved by 1/8 Manchester Regt. Battalion less "A" Coy (attached R.E.) moved to CARDIFF CAMP ST IDESBALD. Weather fine. Casualties Capt. (Revnd) Wild 30R wounded (including 1 at duty)	See Operation Orders No. 27
25.9.17 ST IDESBALD	Battalion less "A" Coy marched to GHYVELDE. Weather fine. Casualties. 5 O.R. wounded (including 1 at duty)	See Operation Orders No. 23?
26.9.17 GHYVELDE	Under Canvas "A" Coy rejoined Battalion. Battalion Training. Weather fine. Casualties – nil	

WAR DIARY or INTELLIGENCE SUMMARY

(Erase heading not required.)

Army Form C. 2118.

Hour, Date, Place	Summary of Events and Information	Remarks and references to Appendices
27.9.17 GHYVELDE	Battalion Training in morning Brigade Training in afternoon Casualties nil	
28.9.17 GHYVELDE	Battalion left by busses for RENESCURE AREA Weather fine Casualties nil	See Operation Order No 39
29.9.17 RENESCURE AREA	Battalion Training Weather fine Casualties nil Battalion in billets	
30.9.17 RENESCURE AREA	Brigade Training Weather fine Casualties nil	

SECRET.

2/8th Batt. Manchester Regiment.

Order No. 35.

Refce. COXYDE 1/20,000.

Copy No. ...5......
2/9/17.

1. The Battalion will be relieved by 2/8th Batt. Lancashire Fusiliers on Wednesday, September 5th 1917.

2. Relief will commence at 9 a.m., and will be complete by 2 p.m.

3. On relief the Battalion will move into quarters at ST. IDESBALDE vacated by 2/5th Batt. East Lancashire Regt. Companies will move independently to ST. IDESBALDE by shortest route. A minimum distance of 200 yards will be kept between platoons.

4. The Transport Officer and the Quartermaster will arrange for removal of Q.M. Stores throughout the day. Transport lines to be clear by 5 a.m.

5. Officers' baggage will be dumped at the Q.M. Stores by 9 a.m.

6. All huts, cookhouses, latrines, etc. are to be left clean.

7. Copies of Battalion Fire Orders will be taken, and posted in new quarters immediately on arrival.

8. Baggage wagons from the Train will report at 5 a.m. at WILTSHIRE CAMP. These wagons will be returned to the Train immediately after move.

9. Completion of relief in WILTSHIRE CAMP will be reported to Batt. H.Q. WILTSHIRE CAMP, and completion of move to Batt. H.Q. ST. IDESBALDE.

10. Transport Lines and Stores in WILTSHIRE CAMP will be taken over by 2/5th Batt. East Lancs. Regt.

11. Acknowledge.

(Signed) A. Westall, 2nd Lieut. & A/Adjt.
2/8th Battalion Manchester Regiment.

Issued at 6 p.m.

Copy No. 1. 199th Infy. Bgde.	Copy No. 9. O.C. "HQ" Coy.
" " 2. 2/8th Batt. Lancs. Fus.	" "10. M.O.
" " 3. 2/5th Batt. East Lancs. Regt.	" "11. T.O.
" " 4. C.O.	" "12. Q.M.
" " 5. O.C. "A" Coy.	" "13. R.S.M.
" " 6. O.C. "B" Coy.	" "14/15. War Diary.
" " 7. O.C. "C" Coy.	" "16. Retained.
" " 8. O.C. "D" Coy.	

S E C R E T

2/6th Battalion Manchester Regiment.

Order No. 26.

Refce :- Coxyde 1/20,000.
Lombartzyde 1/20,000.

Copy No..........
18/9/17.

1. The Battalion will relieve 2/4th East Lancashire Regt. in RIGHT SUB-SECTOR, NIEUPORT BAINS SECTOR on night of 19/20th September 1917.

2. Dispositions in the line will be as follows :-

    Right Coy.............."C" Coy.
    Left Coy..............."B" "
    Close Support........."D" " (Sunken Road).

3. Coys. will march from ST.IDESBALDE in above order. Leading Platoon of "C" Coy. will march at 6 p.m., and 200 yards distance will be maintained between platoons. Route : X Roads W.18.c.5.7. COXYDE - OOST DUNKERKE.

4. Coys. will go into line in strength not exceeding 125 O.R. Details will remain in billets in COXYDE BAINS under 2nd Lieut. PORTER.

5. All maps, aeroplane photos, defence schemes, trench stores, S.A.A., etc. will be taken over, and duplicate receipts sent to Orderly Room by 12 noon the day following relief.

6. Completion of Reliefs will be reported to Battn.H.Q. by runner, using the code word "CHOCK".

7. Transport Lines and Q.M.Stores will be taken over from 2/4th East Lancashire Regt. at X 1 a 2.7. (COXYDE BAINS)

    Baggage wagons will report as follows :-
            19/9/17   4-30 p.m.   3 wagons.
    The wagons will be returned to Train Coy. immediately after move.

8. Acknowledge.

(Sgd) A.Westall, 2nd Lieut.& Adjt.
2/6th Batt.Manchester Regiment.

Issued at 12-30 pm.
Copy No.1....199th INF. BGDE.
 " " 2....2/4th EAST LANCS.
 " " 3....2/5th MANCH.REGT.
 " " 4....Commanding Officer.
 " " 5....O.C. "A" Coy.
 " " 6...." "B" "
 " " 7...." "C" "
 " " 8...." "D" "
 " " 9...." "HQ" "
 " "10....M.O.
 " "11....T.O.
 " "12....Q.M.
 " "13....R.S.M.
 " "14/15..War Diary.
 " "16....Retained.

SECRET.

1/8th Batt. Manchester Regt.

Order No. 37

Refce.- Coyds. 1/...... Copy No. 14
Lombartzyde 1/...... 24/9/17.

1.(a) The Battalion will be relieved by the 1/5th Batt. Manchester Regt. in the RIGHT SUB-SECTOR, NIEUPORT BAINS SECTOR on the night 24th/25th Sept. 1917.

(b) On relief Battalion will move to Cardiff Camp, ST. IDESBALDE.

2. Advance party from relieving Battalion will arrive early morning 24th Sept. Guides will meet this party at R.36.a.85.30. at 6 a.m.

3. Companies on relief will hand over all defence schemes, aeroplane photos, trench maps, anti-aircraft pivot mountings, trench stores, details of work in progress or proposed, and will obtain receipts; copies to reach Batt.H.Q. 9 a.m. 25/9/17. All camps, billets, dug-outs and cellars occupied by Battn. must be left clean and tidy.

4. Companies in line will leave 1 officer and 1 N.C.O. per Coy. with relieving unit for 24 hours after relief.

5. Company attached 184 Tunnelling Coy. will be relieved on Sept. 25th at 10 am, and will rejoin unit at GHYVELDE on relief.

6. Company attached 184 Tunnelling Coy. will take with them rations for day following day of relief.

7. Officer i/c Details will arrange to send billeting party to Area Commandant, ST. IDESBALDE at 1 a.m. 24/9/17, to take over camp and billets.

8. Baggage wagons will report as follows -
   24/9/17 - 8 a.m. 4 wagons at X.L.A.S.D. After move wagons to return immediately to Train Coy.
   Transport Lines and Q.M.Stores to be clear by 2 p.m.

9. 1 Guide per platoon and Batt. and Coy. H.Q. to be at Rd. Junction COST DUNKERKE, R.27.A.35.30 at 7-15 p.m. 24/9/17.

10. The Batt. will move to GHYVELDE on Sept. 25th, commencing 3-30 p.m. Detailed orders will be issued later.

11. Completion of relief to be reported by code word "STUNG".

12. Acknowledge.

(Signed) A. Westall, 2nd Lieut. Adjt.
1/8th Battalion Manchester Regiment.

Issued at 12-30 a.m.
Copy No.1.   18th Inf. Bde.
   "   " 2.   1/5th Bn. Manch. Regt.
   "   " 3.   Commanding Officer.
   "   " 4.   O.C. "A" Coy.
   "   " 5.   "   "B" "
   "   " 6.   "   "C" "
   "   " 7.   "   "D" "
   "   " 8.   "   "HQ" "
   "   " 9.   M.O.
   "   " 10.   Q.M.
   "   " 11.   T.O.
   "   " 12.   R.S.M.
   "   " 13.   War Diary.
   "   " 14.   do.
   "   " 15.   Retained.

SECRET.   2/8th Batt. Manchester Regiment.   Copy No...13.....
                            Order No. 37. 38   25/9/17.

Ref ce - Furnes, 1/40,000.

1. The Battalion will move to GHYVELDE on Sept. 25th 1917.

2. Distances of 200 yds. between Coys. will be maintained in the march.

3. Order of march - "HQ" Coy. - "B" Coy. - "C" Coy. - "D" Coy.

4. HQ. Coy. will move at 4-50 p.m. and will pass the starting point cross roads W.18.c.5.7. at 5-04 p.m.

5. Route - X Roads W.18.c.5.7. - KERKE PANNE - LA PANNE - ADINKERKE - xxxxxxxxxxxxxxxxx PONT DE GHYVELDE.

6. The Batt. will be prepared to leave the XV Corps area on Sept. 28th by bus. Transport will move by road one day previous to the personnel.

7. 2nd Lt. Mawson will remain behind to hand over camp at ST. IDESBALDE.

8. Party attached 184 Tunnelling Coy. will proceed to GHYVELDE on 26/9/17.

9. Acknowledge.

                                            (Sgd) A. Westall, Capt. & Adjt.
                                               2/8th Batt. Manchester Rgt.

Issued at 1 pm.
Copy No. 1. 199 Bde.
  "   " 2. C.O.
  "   " 3. O.C "A" Coy.
  "   " 4. " "B" "
  "   " 5. " "C" "
  "   " 6. " "D" "
  "   " 7. " "HQ" "

Copy No 8 MO
     "   9 QM
     " 10 T.O
     " 11 R.tr
     " 12/13 War Diary
     " 14 Retained

SECRET.	2/8th Batt. Manchester Regiment.	Copy No. 14.
	Order No. 29.	26/9/17.

Refce - Sheet 11 S.E. 1/20,000
    "   10
    "   Hazebrouck 5A. 1/100,000

1. The Battalion will move by bus from GHYVELDE to RENESCURE Area, on Sept. 27th and 28th 1917, in accordance with attached Table "A".

2. Detailed arrangements for embussing will be given in Appendix "B" to be issued later.

3. (a) An Advance party of Lt. Gibbons and Coy. Q.M. Sgts. will travel with 2/8th Bn. Lancs. Fuslrs, embussing at 11-30 a.m. on the GHYVELDE - BRAY DUNES Road, between 2/1st Field Ambulance and 420th Field Coy. R.E., about 400 yards S. of PONT DE GHYVELDE.
   (b) Advance parties will meet their units on arrival at the places of debussing shown in Table "A", and guide them to billeting area.

4. All huts, tents and billets will be left clean.

5. Acknowledge.

Issued at 3 pm.   (Signed) A. Westall, Capt. & Adjt.
                                   2/8th Batt. Manchester Regiment.
Copy No. 1. 19th Bde.
  "   " 2. C.O.   Copy No. 9. M.O.
  "   " 3. 2nd in Commd.   "   " 10. T.O.
  "   " 4. O.C. "A" Coy.   "   " 11. Q.M.
  "   " 5. "   "B" "   "   " 12. R.S.M.
  "   " 6. "   "C" "   "   " 13. War Diary.
  "   " 7. "   "D" "   "   " 14.   do.
  "   " 8. "   "HQ" "   "   " 15. Retained.

W☩ W 8 199/66

2/8th BATT. MANCHESTER REG.

WAR DIARY

OCTOBER 1917

Army Form C. 2118.

WAR DIARY
or
INTELLIGENCE SUMMARY.

(Erase heading not required.)

Instructions regarding War Diaries and Intelligence Summaries are contained in F.S. Regs., Part II. and the Staff Manual respectively. Title pages will be prepared in manuscript.

Hour, Date, Place	Summary of Events and Information	Remarks and references to Appendices
1st Oct 1917 RENESCURE AREA	Battalion training in morning. Brigade training in afternoon. Weather fine. Casualties NIL	
2nd Oct 1917 RENESCURE AREA	Brigade training in the morning. Standing fast for none in the afternoon. Weather fine. Casualties Nil	
3rd Oct 1917 BRANDHOEK ERIE CAMP	Battalion marched from Renescure area to ARQUES and entrained there for BRANDHOEK. Accommodated in huts in ERIE CAMP. Weather showery. Casualties Nil.	Appendix A.1.
4th Oct 1917 BRANDHOEK	Battalion received orders at 6.30 p.m. to move to YPRES SOUTH and marched off at 7.30 p.m. No billets available in YPRES SOUTH and the battalion was accommodated in ruined houses in VLAMERTINGHE. Casualties NIL.	Appendix A.2.
5th Oct 1917 VLAMERTINGHE	Battalion relieved 37th and 38th Regiments Australian Infantry in support outpost line. Very difficult march. Weather stormy. Casualties NIL	
6th Oct 1917 Support Sector D16 c9 & D16 c 9.2 Sheet 28	Situation quiet. Intermittent shelling throughout the day. Casualties 3. Orders received to relieve the right front battalion of the 49th Division immediately on taking up of by battalion. Guide met companies at 9 P.M.	Appendix A.3.

WAR DIARY or INTELLIGENCE SUMMARY

Army Form C. 2118.

Hour, Date, Place	Summary of Events and Information	Remarks and references to Appendices
7th Oct 1917. Left Front Sector. D.10.b.6.3 & D.16.b.4.6 Sheet 28.	Situation fairly active. No continuous trench system. The front line companies occupying shell holes. No overhead cover of any sort. Weather dull. Casualties 5 missing 14.	
8th Oct 1917 do.	Considerable shelling of front line and support company. Advance party from 4th Bn K.O.Y.L.I. to reconnoitre trenches formed to assembly point for assaulting battalions. Heavy shelling around battalion headquarters. Direct hit obtained on runners hut and majority of headquarters signallers and runners became casualties. Weather wet. Casualties 21.	
9th Oct 1917 do.	Assaulting battalions moving up to front of assembly during early hours of morning. Zero hour 5.30 a.m. Many stragglers wandering about the battalion area. A number took shelter in our front line and were sent forward by the C.O. Company information scanty from rheumatism and wounded as to progress of assault sent to Brigade Headquarters accordingly. Communication maintained by Runners. Instructions received from 97th Brigade to stand by ready to	

WAR DIARY
INTELLIGENCE SUMMARY

Army Form C. 2118.

Hour, Date, Place	Summary of Events and Information	Remarks and references to Appendices
9th Oct. 1917 continued	support attack on Final Objective. These instructions were afterwards cancelled by the 199 Bde. who stated that the battalion was under the orders of the 198th Bde. Orders received to cover Personal Front from extreme left (Aden Wood) until touch was obtained with 2/5th Bn (Manchester Regt) on the right. 2/5th Bn Manchester Regt failed to take up position & the battalion covered a front of about 800 yards. Casualties 82.	
10th Oct 1917 Left front sector D10.c.6.3.6 D16.a.4.6. Sheet 28.	Early heavy shelling of battalion area. Advance parties from relieving battalion – 41st Regiment Australian Infantry arrived. Relief complete by 11.30 pm. Casualties 33.	Appendix A. 4.
11th Oct. 1917 BRANDHOEK.	Battalion resting in Brie camp. Men suffering very much from trench feet & exposure generally. The battalion was praised and thanked for their conduct in the line by the G.O.C. Division and G.O.C. Brigade Col. Law 22	

Army Form C. 2118.

WAR DIARY
or
INTELLIGENCE SUMMARY.
(Erase heading not required.)

Instructions regarding War Diaries and Intelligence Summaries are contained in F.S. Regs., Part II. and the Staff Manual respectively. Title pages will be prepared in manuscript.

Hour, Date, Place	Summary of Events and Information	Remarks and references to Appendices
12th Oct 1917 BRANDHOEK	Battalion resting and refitting & having casualties and medical Inspection	
13th Oct 1917. BRANDHOEK.	Battalion entrained for RENESCURE AREA and occupied billets in Mt ARQUES.	Appendix A 5.
14th Oct 1917 ARQUES	Battalion resting. Blank pouches Casualties (wounded)	
15th Oct 1917 ARQUES	Training of specialists and remainder field work	
16th Oct 1917 ARQUES	Training	
17th Oct 1917 ARQUES	Training	
18th Oct 1917 ARQUES	Training	

Army Form C. 2118.

WAR DIARY
or
INTELLIGENCE SUMMARY

(Erase heading not required.)

Instructions regarding War Diaries and Intelligence Summaries are contained in F. S. Regs., Part II. and the Staff Manual respectively. Title pages will be prepared in manuscript.

Hour, Date, Place	Summary of Events and Information	Remarks and references to Appendices
19th Oct. 1917 ARQUES	Batt'n Training weather fine	
20th Oct. 1917 do	Batt'n Training weather fine	
21st Oct. 1917 do	Batt'n Training – Church Parade	
22nd Oct. 1917 do	Batt'n Training – weather fine	
23 Oct 1917 do	Batt'n Training, inspected by Army Commander (Gen'l Plumer)	
24th Oct 1917 do	Batt'n Training weather fine	
25th Oct 1917 do	Batt'n Training weather stormy	
26th Oct 1917 do	Batt'n Training weather stormy	
27th Oct 1917 do	Batt'n Training (night operations)	
28th Oct 1917 do	Church Parade. Several Platoon officers & tent. P.N.Cos of Batt'n have been awarded meritory crosses for conspicuous services in the recent fighting.	

WAR DIARY or **INTELLIGENCE SUMMARY**

Army Form C. 2118.

Hour, Date, Place	Summary of Events and Information	Remarks and references to Appendices
29th Oct 1917 ARQUES	Inspected along with other batts in the 199 Brigade by Sir Douglas Haig. Complimented for smartness of appearance and saluti Weather fine.	
30 Oct 1917 ARQUES	Brigade Training. Practice attack commenced, but discontinued owing to bad weather.	
31 Oct 1917 ARQUES	Presentation by G.O.C. 66th Division of Military Cross to Lieut Hood (C. Co) and 12 Military Medals to men for conspicuous bravery during the recent fighting. Weather fine.	

2/8 Battⁿ Manchester Reg^{mt}

War Diary

Appendices

and

Casualties

for

October 1917

SECRET.

APPENDIX A

2/8th Battalion Manchester Regiment.
Order No. 40.

Copy No 14.
2/10/17.

1. The Battalion will move to BRANDHOEK to-morrow, 3/10/17.

2. The Battalion will entrain at ARQUES at 6-40 a.m.

3. Companies will assemble at the cross-roads at Hdqs. Mess (Coys. halting short of the cross-roads) ready to move off at 4-10 a.m.

4. Dress - F.S.M.O. Steel helmets will be worn.

5. Breakfast - 3 a.m.

6. 2nd Lieut. Porter will report at WARDREQUES SQUARE at 7 a.m. to-morrow. Full instructions will be handed to him at B.H.Q. to-night.

7. Motor Lorries will collect surplus stores at Transport Lines to-morrow morning.

8. The rear party under the Q.M. will accompany the lorries.

9. Billeting Party.- On arrival at BRANDHOEK each Coy and H.Q. Coy. will detail a N.C.O. to report to Lt. Gibbons, who will report with his Party to the Staff Captain's Representative immediately the train arrives at BRANDHOEK.

10. Acknowledge.

(Signed) A. Westall, Capt & Adjt.
2/8th Battn. Manchester Regiment.

Issued at 8 p.m.
Copy No 1. 199th Bde.
"   " 2. C.O.
"   " 3. 2nd in Command.
"   " 4. O.C. "A" Coy.
"   " 5. "   "B" Coy.
"   " 6. "   "C" Coy.
"   " 7. "   "D" Coy.
"   " 8. "   "HQ" Coy.
"   " 9. M.O.
"   " 10. T.O.
"   " 11. Q.M.
"   " 12. R.S.M.
"   " 13. War Diary.
"   " 14.   do.
"   " 15. Retained.

APPENDIX A1

SECRET.   APPENDIX A2

2/8th Battalion, Manchester Regiment.   Copy No.

Refce Sheet 28.   1/40,000.

Order No. 41.

1. The Battalion will move to YPRES SOUTH on the night 4/10/17, and will relieve the 37th and 38th Regiments A.I.F. on the night 5/6th Oct., in the sector D 16 c 0.2 to D 16 c 9.2.

2. The battalion will be in support to the 2/7th Bn. Manchester Regt.
   "C" Coy on the left,
   "D" Coy. on the right,
   "B" Coy. close support,
   "A" Coy. Reserve.

3. Rations for the 6th and 7th Oct., will be carried on the man.

                                (Signed) A. Westall, Capt & Adjt.
   5/10/17.   2/8th Bn. Manchester Regt.

Copy No. 1.	199th Bde.	
" " 2.	C.O.	
" " 3.	2nd in Command.	
" " 4.	O.C. "A" Coy.	
" " 5.	" "B" Coy.	
" " 6.	" "C" Coy.	
" " 7.	" "D" Coy.	
" " 8.	" "H.Q." Coy.	
Copy No 9.	M.O.	
" " 10	T.O.	
" " 11	Q.M.	
" " 12	R.S.M.	
" " 13	War Diary.	
" " 14	do.	
" " 15	Retained.	

APPENDIX A2

APPENDIX A.3

SECRET.   Copy No

2/8th Battn. Manchester Regiment.
            Order No. 42.
        Refce. Sheet 28. 1/40,000

1. The Battalion will relieve the right front battalion of the 49th Division on the night Oct. 6/7th.

2. Guides will meet the Companies on the extreme left of line held by "C" Coy. at 9 p.m.

3. "A" and "C" Coys. will be in the front line.
   "B" Coy. in support.
   "D" Coy. in reserve.

4. The frontage of the Battalion will be from D 10 c 6.8. to D 16 b 4.6.

6/10/17   (Sgd) A. Westall. Capt & Adjt.
                                2/8th Bn. Manchester Regt.

Copy No 1.   199th Bde.
 "   " 2.   C.O.   Copy No 9. M.O.
 "   " 3.   2nd in Command.   "   " 10. T.O.
 "   " 4.   O.C. "A" Coy.   "   " 11. Q.M.
 "   " 5.   "   "B" Coy.   "   " 12. R.S.M.
 "   " 6.   "   "C" Coy.   "   " 13. War Diary.
 "   " 7.   "   "D" Coy.   "   " 14.   do.
 "   " 8.   "   "HQ" Coy.   "   " 15. Retained.

APPENDIX A.3

APPENDIX A4 Copy No.

SECRET

2/8th Battn. Manchester Regiment.

Order No 45.
Refce Sheet 28.

1. The Battalion will be relieved by the 41st Regt A.I.F. on the night 10/11th October.

2. On relief the Battalion will proceed to ERIE CAMP at BRANDHOEK.

3. Coy. Commanders will report completion of relief personally at Battn H.Q.

10/10/17.   (Sgd) A. Westall, Capt & Adjt.
            2/8th Bn. Manchester Regt.

Copy No 1. 199th Bde.
"   "   2. O.C.
"   "   3. 2nd in Command.
"   "   4. O.C. "A" Coy.
"   "   5. O.C. "B" Coy.
"   "   6. O.C. "C" Coy.
"   "   7. O.C. "D" Coy.
"   "   8. O.C. "HQ" Coy.
"   "   9. M.O.
"   " 10. T.O.
"   " 11. Q.M.
"   " 12. R.S.M.
"   " 13. War Diary.
"   " 14.   do.
"   " 15. Retained.

APPENDIX A4

SECRET.

APPENDIX A5

2/8th Battalion Manchester Regt.

Copy No......
12/10/17.

OPERATION ORDER No. 44

1. The Battalion moves to RENESCURE Area to-morrow.

2. Companies will parade facing West, ready to move off at 6-30 a.m. in the following order.
   "B" Coy. "C" Coy. "D" Coy. "A" Coy. "HQ" Coy.

3. Dress F.S.M.O. Steel Helmets.
   Each man will carry one blanket, and if wet groundsheet round the shoulders.
   The remaining blankets are to be rolled in bundles of 10 outside the Q.M. Stores by 5-30 a.m.

4. Breakfast 5 a.m.

5. Officers' valises and Coy. boxes will be at Q.M. Stores at 6 a.m.

6. Transport will move G.S. Wagons at 7 a.m. by road.
   Remainder will entrain at VLAMERTINGHE at 8 a.m.

7. Company Commanders are responsible that the lines are left clean.

(Sgd) A. Westall, Capt. & Adjt.
2/8th Batt. Manchester Regt.

Copy No. 1.	O.C. 199th Inf. Bde.			
" " 2.	Commandg. Officer.		Copy No. 11.	R.S.M.
" " 3.	2nd in Command		" " 12.	War Diary.
" " 4.	O.C. "A" Coy.		" " 13.	do.
" " 5.	" "B" Coy.		" " 14.	Retained
" " 6.	" "C" Coy			
" " 7.	" "D" Coy.			
" " 8.	T.O.			
" " 9.	M.O.			
" " 10.	Q.M.			

APPENDIX A5

Army Form C. 2118.

WAR DIARY
or
INTELLIGENCE SUMMARY

(Erase heading not required.)

Instructions regarding War Diaries and Intelligence Summaries are contained in F. S. Regs., Part II. and the Staff Manual respectively. Title pages will be prepared in manuscript.

Hour, Date, Place	Summary of Events and Information	Remarks and references to Appendices

Total Casualties for Oct 1917

OFFICERS		OTHER RANKS	
KILLED	WOUNDED	KILLED	WOUNDED AND SICK
1	7	44	145

NIL - MISSING

5/8th Batt. Manchester Regt.

CASUALTIES FOR OCTOBER 1917.

1st. Oct. 1917.	... ...	Nil.
2nd " "	,,, ,,,	Nil.
3rd " "	... ...	Nil.
4th " "	... ...	Nil.
5th " "	,,, ,,,	Nil.
6th " "	,,, ,,,	Wounded - Other Ranks 3.
7th " "	... ...	Wounded - Other Ranks 5, including 1 at duty. Missing - Other Ranks 14.
8th " "	,,, ...	Killed - Other Ranks 3. Wounded - Officers; Capt.R.WHITWORTH(8th) 2nd Lt.F.DICKINSON (8th); 2nd.Lt. R.STOCKDALE (8th). Other Ranks 14.
9th " "	... ...	Killed - Other Ranks 23. Wounded - Officers; Capt.R.C.BARDSLEY (8th) Lieut.W.GIBBONS (8th). Other Ranks 57. Missing - Other Ranks 8.
10th " "	,,, ,,,	Killed - Other Ranks 13. Wounded - Other Ranks 30. Missing - Other Ranks 3.
11th " "	... ...	Killed - Other Ranks 4. Wounded - Other Ranks 17. Missing - Other Ranks 20.
12th " "	... ...	8 Other Ranks reported missing 11th now reported wounded. 6 Other Ranks reported missing 11th now rejoined 12th.
13th " "	... ...	1 Other Rank reported killed 9th now reported wounded. 5 Other Ranks reported missing 7th now reported wounded. 5 Other Ranks reported missing 7th rejoined 13th.
14th " "	... ...	Wounded - Other Ranks 1 (Accidental).
15th " "	... ...	Nil.
16th " "	... ...	2nd Lt.PORTER,N.P. and 2nd Lt.ROBINSON,K. now reported wounded 11th. 2 Other Ranks reported missing 11th now rejoined. 3 Other Ranks reported missing 10th now reported wounded.
17th " "	... ...	Wounded - Other Ranks 1. 1 Other Rank reported missing 11th rejoined 16th. 2 Other Ranks reported missing 7th now found to be sick in Hospital.

(1)

18th Oct.1917	Nil.
19th " "	1 Other Rank reported missing 11th, now reported sick in hospital.
20th " "	Nil.
21st " "	Nil.
22nd " "	Nil.
23rd " "	1 Other rank reported missing 9th now believed killed.
24th " "	Nil.
25th " "	1 Other Rank reported missing 7th now reported sick in hospital.
26th " "	Nil.
27th " "	Nil. 1 Other rank reported missing 10th now believed killed. Three Other Ranks reported missing 9th now found to be sick in hospital. 2 Other Ranks reported missing 11th now found to be sick in hospital.
28th " "	Nil.
29th " "	Nil.
30th " "	Nil.
31st " "	Nil.

WAR DIARY

NOVEMBER 1917

2/8 Batt'n Manchester Reg't

Army Form C. 2118.

WAR DIARY
or
INTELLIGENCE SUMMARY.
(Erase heading not required.)

Instructions regarding War Diaries and Intelligence Summaries are contained in F.S. Regs., Part II. and the Staff Manual respectively. Title pages will be prepared in manuscript.

Hour, Date, Place	Summary of Events and Information	Remarks and references to Appendices
November 1st 1917 Ht AROUES	Batt on March from Ht AROUES to LONGUE-CROIX area, Company billets very much scattered N'th and S'th the main road from STAPLE	Appendix A.1.
November 2nd 1917 LONGUE-CROIX	A.B.C. Companies move to fresh billets N'th of STAPLE - LONGUE CROIX road. D Co remain in original billets	
November 3rd 1917 LONGUE-CROIX	All Companies take heads at STAPLE for bath. Specialist training	
November 4th 1917 LONGUE-CROIX	Church Parade	
November 5th 1917 LONGUE-CROIX	The Batt'n in Conjunction with 7/4 manoeuvre practice Assembly preparatory to an attack, also the attack.	

Army Form C. 2118.

WAR DIARY
or
INTELLIGENCE SUMMARY.
(Erase heading not required.)

Instructions regarding War Diaries and Intelligence Summaries are contained in F. S. Regs., Part II. and the Staff Manual respectively. Title pages will be prepared in manuscript.

Hour, Date, Place	Summary of Events and Information	Remarks and references to Appendices
November 6th 1917 LONGUE-CROIX	The Batt'n along with other Batt'ns of the 199 Brigade made a practice attack on a village under the supervision of G.O.C. 199 Brigade	
November 7th 1917 LONGUE-CROIX	The Batt'n along with other Batt'ns of 199 Brigade go on a Route March	
November 8th 1917 LONGUE-CROIX	Company and Specialist Training	
November 9th 1917 LONGUE-CROIX	Batt'n entrains at ESSLINGHEM for ANDERSON and marches to KINORA (VICTORIA) Camp. Sheet 28 M 3. c 9 6	Appendix A 2
November 10th 1917 KINORA M 3. c.9.6.	Specialist Training	

Army Form C. 2118.

WAR DIARY
or
INTELLIGENCE SUMMARY.
(Erase heading not required.)

Instructions regarding War Diaries and Intelligence Summaries are contained in F. S. Regs., Part II and the Staff Manual respectively. Title pages will be prepared in manuscript.

Hour, Date, Place	Summary of Events and Information	Remarks and references to Appendices
November 11th 1917 Winters A 3. c. 9.6.	Batt. to march to Kempton Camp. Field 28 M.14 V.	Appendix A. 3
November 12th 1917 Kempton M.14 V.	Batt. to march to Scottish Lines. Field 28 H.23.5.5. A. B. C. Co's billeted in Scottish Lines. D Co billeted in Dominion Lines. Rifle inspection in afternoon.	Appendix A. 4
November 13th 1917 Scottish Lines H.23.55	Company & Specialist Training	
November 14th 1917 Scottish Lines H.23.55	Company & Specialist Training	
November 15th 1917 Scottish Lines H.23.55	Batt. to march to Montreal Camp. Field 28 H.19 b 4.7 Batt. in Training and Sports in afternoon	Appendix A. 5

WAR DIARY or INTELLIGENCE SUMMARY.

(Erase heading not required.)

Army Form C. 2118.

Hour, Date, Place	Summary of Events and Information	Remarks and references to Appendices
November 16 1917 MONTREAL CAMP H 19. 6. 4. 7	Inspection of hats by Divisional Gas Officer. The usual Bath + Café laid on afternoon at Maritime Camp	
November 17 1917 MONTREAL CAMP H 19 6 4 7	Company + Specialist Training Organised Sports	
November 18 1917 MONTREAL CAMP	Church Parade Cross-Country Run	
November 19 1917 MONTREAL CAMP	Bn. moved to YPRES. Hedquarters & Company + Lewis Gunners billeted in INFANTRY BARRACKS. D Co billeted in GORDON area on working parties A + D Cos billeted on RAILWAY WOOD Bn. out applying working parties.	Appendix A.G
November 20 1917 YPRES.	Headquarters Co. C Company + Lewis Gunners training. A.B + D. Cos supplying working parties. One casualty.	

Army Form C. 2118.

WAR DIARY
or
INTELLIGENCE SUMMARY.
(Erase heading not required.)

Instructions regarding War Diaries and Intelligence Summaries are contained in F. S. Regs., Part II. and the Staff Manual respectively. Title pages will be prepared in manuscript.

Hour, Date, Place	Summary of Events and Information	Remarks and references to Appendices
November 21st 1917 YPRES	Headquarters Coys Gunners & Bombers training. C Coy repairing road A.13 & D Coy supplying working parties.	Appendix A.7
November 22nd 1917 MONTREAL CAMP YPRES	Batt'n march to MONTREAL CAMP H.19 & 4.7.	
November 23rd 1917 MONTREAL CAMP	Company Training. Batt'n took baths at HALIFAX CAMP.	Appendix A.8
November 24th 1917 BERTHEN AREA	Batt'n march to and occupy huts in BERTHEN area.	
November 25th 1917 BERTHEN AREA.	Church Parade.	
November 26th 1917 BERTHEN AREA	Batt'n march to and occupy huts in CAESTRE AREA.	Appendix A.9

Army Form C. 2118.

WAR DIARY
or
INTELLIGENCE SUMMARY.
(Erase heading not required.)

Hour, Date, Place	Summary of Events and Information	Remarks and references to Appendices
November 27 1917 CAESTRE	Company in Specialist Training organised Sports	
November 28 1917 CAESTRE	Company in Specialist Training organised Sports.	
November 29 1917 CAESTRE	Company in Specialist Training organised Sports.	
November 30 1917	Company in Specialist Training organised Sports. Casualties for November 1917 The O.R. wounded	

APPENDICES AND CASUALTY

RETURN FOR NOVEMBER 1917

2/8 Batt'n MANCHESTER Reg't.

2/8th Batt. Manchester Regt.

Casualties for month of November 1917.

```
Nov. 1st 1917..........Nil.
  "  2nd   "   ..........Nil.
  "  3rd   "   ..........Nil.
  "  4th   "   ..........Nil.
  "  5th   "   ..........Nil.
  "  6th   "   ..........Nil.
  "  7th   "   ..........Nil.
  "  8th   "   ..........Nil.
  "  9th   "   ..........Nil.
  " 10th   "   ..........Nil.
  " 11th   "   ..........Nil.
  " 12th   "   ..........Nil.
  " 13th   "   ..........Nil.
  " 14th   "   ..........2nd Lt. K. Robinson previously reported "Wounded"
                         8/10/17, now reported NOT wounded.
  " 15th   "   ..........Nil.
  " 16th   "   ..........Nil.
  " 17th   "   ..........Nil.
  " 18th   "   ..........Nil.
  " 19th   "   ..........Nil.
  " 20th   "   ..........Wounded 1 other rank.
  " 21st   "   ..........Nil.
  " 22nd   "   ..........Nil.
  " 23rd   "   ..........Nil.
  " 24th   "   ..........Nil.
  " 25th   "   ..........Nil.
  " 26th   "   ..........Nil.
  " 27th   "   ..........Nil.
  " 28th   "   ..........Nil.
  " 29th   "   ..........Nil.
  " 30th   "   ..........Nil.
```

SECRET.　　　　　　　2/8th Battalion Manchester Regiment.　　Copy No........
　　　　　　　　　　　　　　Order No. 45.

Ref. Map Sheet 27, 1/40,000.

1. The Battn will move to WALLON CAPPEL Area (STAPLE Sub-area) on Nov 1st. 1917.

2. The Batt. will parade at 1-30 p.m.
   "HQ" Coy, "A" Coy, and "B" Coy, parade outside Battn H.Q.
   "C" and "D" Coys parade outside their billets, facing S.W.
   A distance of 200 yards will be maintained between Coys, and between rear Coy. and Transport.

3. 1st Line Transport will accompany the Battn.

4. 2nd. Line Baggage Wagons will report at Q.M. Stores at 7-30 a.m. They will march with train, and be formed into a convoy on the ARQUES- HAZEBROUCK Road, at road junction S.17.c.75.79., by 10 am. They will leave Q.M. Stores not later than 9-30 a.m.

5. 1 Motor Lurry (No.5) will report at Q.M. Stores at 6-15 a.m. This will be loaded, and will report to an officer of Bde H.Qs at road junction, S.17.c.75.79. at 10-30 a.m. This Motor Lurry will return to Q.M. Stores for a second load.
   Q.M. will detail 1 N.C.O. and 4 men to accompany the motor lurry.
   Q.M. will detail a guide to be at the Square, ARQUES, at 8 a.m. to conduct motor lurry to Q.M. Stores.

6. Q.M. will detail 1 N.C.O. to attend at Refilling Point at 8 a.m. Rations for consumption on Novr 2nd will be loaded on train wagons and delivered to units on arrival.

7. Lieut. C.C.Lorenzen and the C.Q.M.S. of each Company will report to Staff Captain at Bde Hdqtrs at 8-15 a.m. They will proceed to ~~Area Commandants Office, STAPLE, and await arrival of remainder of billeting party~~ by bus.

8. Sergt Billings and 1 man per Coy on bicycles will report to Staff Captain at BdeHQ at 7-15 a.m. They will proceed to Area Commandant's Office, STAPLE, and await the arrival of remainder of billeting party.

9. Officers' kits and all Coy stores will be dumped at Q.M. Stores at 6-30 a.m.
   Blankets will be rolled in bundles of 10, and securely tied, and dumped at Q.M. Stores by 7-30 a.m. ("A" Coy by 8 a.m.).

10. Billets to be vacated by 1-15 p.m. All billets and ground in the vicinity must be left scrupulously clean.
    The 2nd in Command and M.O. will inspect billets at 1-15 p.m.

11. Dress - F.S.M.O.; shrapnel helmets.

12. Acknowledge.
　　　　　　　　　　　　　(Signed) G.McDougall,Capt. & Adjt.
　　　　　　　　　　　　　　　　2/8th Bn. Manchester Regiment.

DISTRIBUTION.
Copy No 1. 199th Inf. Bde.　　　　Copy No 9. M.O.
　"　　"　2. Commanding Officer.　　"　　"　10 T.O.
　"　　"　3. 2nd. in Command.　　　　"　　"　11 Q.M.
　"　　"　4. O.C. "A" Coy.　　　　　 "　　"　12 R.S.M.
　"　　"　5. "   "B" "　　　　　　 "　　"　13/18 War Diary.
　"　　"　6. "   "C" "
　"　　"　7. "   "D" "
　"　　"　8. "   H.Q. "

APPENDIX A.1.

SECRET.   Copy No. 14

2/8th Battalion Manchester Regiment.
Order No 4?.

                                                           8/11.17.

Reference Map Sheets 27 and 28. 1/40,000

1. The 199th Infantry Brigade Group (less Transport) will entrain at EBBLINGHEM and detrain at OUDERDOM on Nov. 9th.

2. The Battalion will march to EBBLINGHEM Station in the following order:
   R.Q., "A" Coy., "B" Coy., "C" Coy., "D" Coy.
   Starting Point X roads H.6.c.   LONGUE CROIX.
   Head of Column will pass the starting point at   a.m.
   Route - LONGUE CROIX - X-roads H.   EBBLINGHEM.
   100 yards distance will be maintained between Companies.
   Dress - F.S.M.O., with shrapnel helmets.

3. One blanket will be carried on the man, neatly folded behind the pack

4. Officers' kits and Company mess buckets and cooking utensils will be dumped for loading at Q.M. Stores at 8-30 a.m.

5. One lorry has been allotted to the Battalion for the purpose of carrying stores, cooking utensils, etc. One blanket per man will be carried on the lorry, which will make two journeys.
   The Q.M. will send a guide to Bde.H.Q. at 7.45 a.m. on the 9th inst. to conduct lorry to Q.M. Stores. An unloading party of a N.C.O. and four men will be detailed by Q.M. to accompany the lorry.
   N.C.O. in charge of lorry will report to an Officer detailed by Brigade at X-roads LONGUE CROIX, H.6.c.7.4,   at 10 a.m.
   Lorry will proceed in convoy to the Area Commandant's office, WESTOUTRE, where it will be met by guide from the advanced billeting party.
   Every effort must be made to get the lorry unloaded and returned without undue delay.

6. The unconsumed portion of the day's ration for 9th inst. will be carried on the man.
   Rations for 10th inst will be delivered by train wagons on 9th inst in the WESTOUTRE Area.

7. Guides from the advanced billeting party will meet the Battalion at the Station, OUDERDOM, at 6 p.m.

8. All billets and ground in the vicinity must be left scrupulously clean. O.C. Coys. will inspect their billets before leaving, and render a certificate to the Orderly Room that they have been left clean.

9. Entrainment States to be rendered to Orderly Room by 10 a.m.

10. Acknowledge.

                                    (Signed) G.McDougall, Capt & Adjt.
                                            2/8th Bn. Manchester Regt.

DISTRIBUTION.
Copy No 1. 199th Inf.Bde.
 "   " 2. Commanding Officer.
 "   " 3. 2nd in Command.   Copy No 9. Q.M. & T.O.
 "   " 4. O.C. "A" Coy.   "   " 10. M.O.
 "   " 5. O.C. "B" Coy.   "   " 11. R.S.M.
 "   " 6. O.C. "C" Coy.   "   " 12/14 War Diary.
 "   " 7. O.C. "D" Coy.   "   " 15. Spare.
 "   " 8. O.C. H.Q. Coy.

APPENDIX A. 2

SECRET

3/8th Battalion Manchester Regiment.

Copy No......
10/11/17.

Order No. 47.

Ref. Map Sheet 28. 1/40,000.

1. The Battalion will move to KEMPTON CAMP, M.14.b.4.6. to-morrow.

2. Battalion will march from Camp in the following order:-
   H.Q. Coy.; "A" Coy; "B" Coy; "C" Coy; and "D" Coy.
   H.Q. will leave Camp entrance at 9 a.m.
   200 yards distance will be maintained between Companies.

3. The Q.M. and Transport Officer will arrange for removal of stores to KEMPTON CAMP during the day.
   Blankets (two per man) will be carried on the men.

4. Officers' kits, Coy. boxes etc will be dumped ready for loading at Q.M. Stores by 8-30 a.m.

5. All huts, tents, and lines must be left scrupulously clean. The Medical Officer will inspect the lines at 9 a.m.

6. Acknowledge.

(Signed) G. McDougall, Capt. & Adjt.
Issued at 9-30 p.m.
3/8th Bn. Manchester Regiment.

DISTRIBUTION.

Copy No. 1. 199th. Inf. Brigade.	Copy No 9. M.O.
" " 2. Comdg. Officer.	" " 10. T.O.
" " 3. 2nd in Command.	" " 11. Q.M.
" " 4. O.C. "A" Coy.	" " 12. R.S.M.
" " 5. O.C. "B" Coy.	" " 13/15 War Diary.
" " 6. O.C. "C" Coy.	" " 16 Spare.
" " 7. O.C. "D" Coy.	
" " 8. O.C. H.Q. Coy.	

APPENDIX A.27

S E C R E T.   Copy No.....
                  2/8th Battalion Manchester Regiment,   11/11/17.
                              Order No 48.

Ref. Sheet 28.1/40,000.

1. The Battalion will move to DOMINION LINES (G.24.b.central) La-Terror.

2. Starting Point K.18.b.8.8. (approx., entrance to KEMMEL CAMP.)

3. Route: WESTOUTRE - RIVEREN - SCHERPENEST - X-roads G.25.b.6.4. -
   Cross-roads G.24.c.N.E., where guides will meet Companies.

4. Order of march: H.Q., "B" Coy, "C" Coy, "D" Coy, "A" Coy., Transport.
   Time of passing starting point will be notified later.

5. Distances: 200 yards between Companies and 200 yards between
   A and B portion Transport.

6. Time for Officers' kits, Coy. boxes, etc. to be at H.Q.Stores to
   be notified later.

7. Water bottles will be filled before leaving KEMMEL CAMP.
   Blankets (one per man) will be carried neatly folded under the
   groundsheet on the pack.

8. All huts, tents, lines, etc. will be left scrupulously clean. Coy.
   Officers will inspect their own lines before leaving CAMP.

9. Acknowledge.

Issued at 9 p.m.
                                           (Sgd) G.McCargill,Capt.& Adjt.
DISTRIBUTION.   2/8th Batt,Manchester Regiment.
Copy No. 1 199th Inf.Bd.
  "   " 2. Comdg.Officer.
  "   " 3. 2nd in Command.
  "   " 4. O.C. "A" Coy.
  "   " 5. O.C. "B" Coy.
  "   " 6. O.C. "C" Coy.
  "   " 7. O.C. "D" Coy.
  "   " 8. O.C. "H Q" Coy.
  "   " 9. M.O.
  "   " 10. Q.M.
  "   " 11. T.O.
  "   " 12. R.S.M.
  "   " 13/14 War Diary.
  "   " 15. Spare.

APPENDIX. A.4.

1/10th Bn. Manchester Regt.

Addendum to Order No.46.   Copy No..........
                                            .../.../17.

1. Blankets (one per man) will be rolled in bundles of 10, securely tied and, and placed outside the Q.M.Stores by 8 a.m. Officers' kits, company boxes, etc. to be placed outside the Q.M.Stores by 8.30 a.m.

2. Starting Time - 9.30 a.m.

3. Dress - F.S.M.O. - Shrapnel helmets.

                    Sgd. G.McDougall,Capt.& Adjt.
                    1/10th Bn.,Manchester Regiment.

DISTRIBUTION.
Copy No. 1. O. in C. Bn. Hd.Qrs.
   "   " 2. O.sig.Officer.
   "   " 3. 2nd in Command.
   "   " 4. O.C."A" Coy.
   "   " 5.   " "B" "
   "   " 6.   " "C" "
   "   " 7.   " "D" "
   "   " 8. M.O.
   "   " 10. Q.M.
   "   " 11. T.O.
   "   " 12. R.S.M.
   "   " 13. War Diary.
   "   " 14.   "   "
   "   " 15.   "   "
   "   " 16. Spare.

APPENDIX A4.

SECRET. 2/8th Battalion Manchester Regiment.   Copy No. ....
                                                14/11/17.
                Order No. 49.

Reference Sheet 28, 1/40,000.

1. The Battalion will move to MONTREAL CAMP, H.19.b, to-morrow, the 15th inst.

2. Order of march will be as follows:-
   H.Q., "C" Coy., "A" Coy., "B" Coy., "D" Coy.

   Starting Point (except "D" Coy.): On Road at G.23.a.8.6.
   Starting Time: 9-30 a.m.

   "D" Coy. will be at X-roads, G.29.b.5.6. at 9-40 a.m., and take their place in the column in rear of "B" Coy.

3. A distance of 200 yards will be maintained between Companies on the march.

4. All huts and lines to be left scrupulously clean. Huts to be vacated by 9 a.m.

5. The M.O. will inspect huts and lines at 9 a.m.

6. Blankets (1 per man) to be rolled in bundles of 10, securely tied, and dumped for loading near Y.M.C.A. Hut by 8 a.m.

7. Officers' kits and Coy. boxes to be dumped for loading near Y.M.C.A. Hut by 9 a.m.

8. The Transport Officer will place Lewis Gun limbers (less "D" Coy's) on road near M.A. at G.23.x.8.6.x at 8 a.m. Os.C. Companies will arrange to load these limbers without delay.
   "D" Coy. L.G. limber will be loaded at Transport Lines by 8-30 a.m.

9. Q.M. and T.O. will arrange for removal of Stores to MONTREAL CAMP during the day.

10. Dress - F.S.M.O. with shrapnel helmets and 1 blanket per man.

11. Acknowledge.

                                (Signed) G. McDougall, Capt. & Adjt.
14/11/17.   2/8th Battn. Manchester Regt.

DISTRIBUTION.
   Copy No 1. 199th Inf. Bde.
    "   2. Commanding Officer.
    "   3. 2nd. in Command.
    "   4. O.C. "A" Coy.
    "   5.   "   "B" Coy.
    "   6.   "   "C" Coy.
    "   7.   "   "D" Coy.
    "   8.   "   "H.Q. Coy.
    "   9. Q.M.
    "   10. T.O.
    "   11. M.O.
    "   12. R.S.M.
    "   13/15 War Diary.
    "   16. Spare.

APPENDIX A 5

2/8th Battalion Manchester Regiment.

SECRET.

Order No. 50.

Ref. Sheet 28, 1/40,000.

Copy No.....
18/11/17.

1. The Battalion will relieve the 2/4th Bn. West Lancashire Regiment in the GORDON and RAILWAY WOOD Areas.

2. **Dispositions.**

   Headquarters, "C" coy., and Lewis Gun Classes of "A", "B", and "D" Coys. will relieve the Coys. of the 2/4th Bn. West Lancashire Regt. in INFANTRY BARRACKS, YPRES.

   "A" and "D" Coys. (less Lewis Gun Classes) will relieve the 2 Coys. of the 2/4th Bn. West Lancashire Regt. in RAILWAY DUGOUTS.

   "B" Coy. (less Lewis Gun Class) will relieve the Coy. of the 2/4th Bn. West Lancashire Regt. in GORDON AREA near MENIN GATE.

   Transport and Quartermasters Stores will take over from the 2/7th Bn. Lancashire Fusiliers near BELGIAN CHATEAU at about H.23.a.

   Companies will take over working parties from the Companies of the 2/4th Bn. West Lancashire Regt. whom they relieve.

   O.C. "A" Coy. will detail 2 Officers and 2 N.C.Os., and O.C. "D" Coy. 2 Officers and 2 N.C.Os to report to R.E. Officer at BELGIAN BATTERY CORNER at 5 a.m. to-morrow. This party will be responsible for taking over details of work.

   For tactical purposes "A" and "D" Coys. are under the orders of the G.O.C. 198th Brigade, and for this purpose Capt. Westall is in charge of these Coys. He will report personally on arrival of "A" and "D" Coys. at RAILWAY DUGOUTS to G.O.C. 198th Brigade at RAILWAY DUGOUT, at D.26.a.1.3. He will also detail 2 runners to be permanently at Headquarters of the 198th Brigade.

   For purposes of working parties, "A", "B" and "D" Coys. are under the direction of the R.Es., and Officers in charge of working parties are reminded that they are personally responsible for the work being efficiently carried out.

3. **Route.**

   "A" and "D" Coys. - Road junction H.14.b.4.8. - X Roads H.16.d.2.2.
   - Road junction at BELGIAN BATTERY CORNER - YPRES - MENIN GATE (I.8.b.3.1.) - HELL FIRE CORNER (I.10.c.9.2.) - RAILWAY DUGOUTS (I.11.b.about).

   Headquarters, "B" and "C" Coys. - Road junction H.14.b.4.8. - X Roads H.16.d.2.2. - Road junction at BELGIAN BATTERY CORNER - YPRES.

4. **Distances.**

   "A" and "D" Coys. will move from MONTREAL CAMP at 6 a.m.
   Headquarters, "B" and "C" Coys. will move from MONTREAL CAMP at 9 a.m.

   200 yards between Coys. up to X Roads, H.16.d.2.2.; thence by platoons, 100 yards interval between platoons. All traffic regulations to be strictly adhered to in passing through YPRES. Beyond YPRES by sections.

5. Water bottles will be filled, and haversack rations for "A", "B" and "D" Coys. will be carried. 1 blanket will be carried on the man.

   Lewis Gun Limbers will accompany Companies, and will be immediately sent back to Transport Lines near BELGIAN CHATEAU on being unloaded.

2/8th Batt. Manchester Regt.
Order No. 50 (Continued).

Rations for "A" and "D" Coys. will be delivered to BIRR X ROADS at about 3 o'clock.
Rations for "B" Coy. at the MENIN GATE at about 3 o'clock.

6. Officers' valises, Company mess baskets, etc. to be at Q.M. Stores by 8 a.m. prompt.

7. Dress - F.S.M.O.; shrapnel helmets.

8. Huts and lines will be left in a scrupulously clean condition. The Medical Officer will inspect the Camp at 8-30 a.m.

9. Relief Complete.
"Relief Complete" will be immediately reported by runner to Battalion Headquarters.

10. Acknowledge.

                    (Signed) G. McDougall, Capt. & Adjt.
                    2/8th Battalion Manchester Regt.

Issued at 9 p.m.

DISTRIBUTION.
Copy No.	1.	199th Inf. Bde.
"	" 2.	198th Inf. Bde.
"	" 3.	2/4th Bn. East Lancashire Regt.
"	" 4.	2/7th Bn. Lancashire Fusiliers.
"	" 5.	Commanding Officer.
"	" 6.	Second in Command.
"	" 7.	O.C. "A" Coy.
"	" 8.	" "B" "
"	" 9.	" "C" "
"	"10.	" "D" "
"	"11.	" "HQ" "
"	"12.	M.O.
"	"13.	T.O.
"	"14.	Q.M.
"	"15.	R.S.M.
"	16/18	War Diary.
"	19.	Spare.

APPENDIX A.6.

SECRET.

2/6th Batt. Manchester Regt.

Order No. 51.

Ref - Sheet 28, 1/40,000.   Copy No..........
                                              8/11/17.

1. The Battalion, less "A" and "D" Coys., will move to MONTREAL CAMP to-morrow, 9/11/17.

2. Order of March :-
          "B"
          "C" Coy.
          "D" Coy.

   Starting Point - INFANTRY BARRACKS.

   Starting Time - 7-30 a.m.

3. ROUTE :- Road junction BELGIAN BATTERY CORNER - X ROADS
             - I.18.d.3.3. - Road junction H.14.b.4.4.

4. "A" and "D" Coys. will continue work until noon on that inst., then march independently to MONTREAL CAMP. Route - as in para 3.

   Distances. By sections at 10 yards interval to YPRES, thence by platoons at 100 yards interval.

5. The Transport Officer will arrange for L.G.Limbers of "A" and "D" Coys. to report at RAILWAY DUGOUTS at 12 noon. These limbers will accompany the Companies to MONTREAL CAMP.
   Transport Officer will arrange for L.G.Wagons of "B" and "C" Coys., 1 limbered wagon for H.Q. and the mess cart to report at INFANTRY BARRACKS, YPRES, at 7-10 a.m.
   When loaded, L.G.Wagons of "B" and "C" Coys. will return once to transport lines.

6. Officers' kits to be dumped ready for loading at entrance to INFANTRY BARRACKS at 7-45 a.m.
   Officers will arrange for their own batmen to load their kits.

7. All barrack rooms, dugouts, cookhouses, latrines, and adjacent ground must be left scrupulously clean.
   Medical Officer will inspect the Barracks at 9 a.m.

8. Dress :- F.S.M.O., shrapnel helmets, one Blanket.

9. Acknowledge.

                      (Signed) A.McDougall, Capt. & Adjt.
                              2/6th Battalion Manchester Regiment.

   Issued at   p.m.

DISTRIBUTION.
Copy No. 1.   199th Inf.Bde.
  "   " 2.   Commanding Officer.
  "   " 3.   2nd in Command.
  "   " 4.   O.C. "A" Coy.
  "   " 5.   "B" "
  "   " 6.   "C" "
  "   " 7.   "D" "
  "   " 8.   "HQ" "
  "   " 9.   M.O.
  "   " 10.   T.O.
  "   " 11.   Q.M.
  "   " 12.   R.S.M.

APPENDIX A. 7

SECRET.　　　　　　2/8th Battalion Manchester Regiment.　　　　Copy No......
　　　　　　　　　　　　　　　Order No. 52.

Ref. Sheets No.27 & 28., 1/40,000.

1. The Battalion will move to the BERTHEN area to-morrow.

2. Head of column will pass X Roads, H.19.b.4.7. at 8-10 a.m.

3. Order of March.- Signallers & Headquarters Coy.
　　　　　　　　　　Band.
　　　　　　　　　　"D" Coy.
　　　　　　　　　　"A" Coy.
　　　　　　　　　　"B" Coy.
　　　　　　　　　　"C" Coy.

4. Distances.- 200 yards between Coys.

5. Transport will march with unit.

6. Route.- ZEVECOTEN - RENINGHELST - WESTOUTRE (M.9.c.3.5.) - M.8.c.1.3 - X Roads R.16.c. - BERTHEN - to Billet area X.1.a.

7. Guides will meet Companies and Transport at X Roads BERTHEN, R.22.c.6.8.

8. Dinners will be issued after arrival at billets. Coy. Commanders will arrange for their dinners to be ready when the field kitchens arrive.

9. Turn out.- The greatest care is to be taken to ensure men being well and uniformly turned out. No sandbags or parcels are to be carried. Ration bags, plates and mugs must be inside the pack or haversack.

10. All points of march discipline are to be carefully observed during the march and at the halts.

11. Dress.- F.S.M.O.; shrapnel helmets.

12. All huts will be vacated by 7-40 a.m., and the huts and the lines are to be left scrupulously clean.

13. The 2nd in Command and the M.O. will inspect the Camp at 7-45 a.m.

14. Acknowledge.

　　　　　　　　　　　　　　　　　　(Signed) G. McDougall, Capt.& Adjt.
　　　　　　　　　　　　　　　　　　　　　　2/8th Bn. Manchester Regt.

23/11/17.

Issued at 7-30 p.m.

APPENDIX A 8

DISTRIBUTION.
Copy No.　1. 199th Inf. Bde.
　"　　"　2. Commanding Officer.
　"　　"　3. 2nd. in Command.
　"　　"　4. O.C. "A" Coy.
　"　　"　5.　"　 "B"　"
　"　　"　6.　"　 "C"　"
　"　　"　7.　"　 "D"　"
　"　　"　8.　"　 H.Q.　"
　"　　"　9.　"　 Q.M.
　"　　"　10.　"　 T.O.
　"　　"　11. M.O.
　"　　"　12. R.S.M.
　"　　"　13/15. War Diary.
　"　　"　16.- Spare.

S E C R E T.

2/8th Battalion Manchester Regiment.
Order No.51.

Copy No......

Ref. Sheet No.27.1/40,000 Belgium & France.

1. The Battalion will move to CAESTRE area to-morrow.

2. Head of the column will pass Road junction point X.7.b.7.4. at 11 a.m.

3. Order of March: Headquarters Coy, Band, "A", "B", "C", "D", Transport.

4. Distances: 200 yards between Companies.

5. Transport will march with unit.

6. Route: FLETRE - CAESTRE.

7. Guides will meet Companies at CAESTRE, Road junction W.8.a.8.5.

8. Dinners will be issued after arrival in billets. Coy Commanders will arrange to have dinners ready by 1-30 p.m.

9. Turn out: The greatest care is to be taken to ensure men being well and uniformly turned out. No sandbags or parcels are to be carried. Ration bags, plates and mugs must be inside the pack or haversack.

10. All points of march discipline are to be carefully observed during the march and at the halts.

11. Dress: F.S.M.O.; shrapnel helmets.

12. All billets will be vacated by 10 a.m. (unless it is raining hard) and billets and land in the vicinity left scrupulously clean.

13. The 2nd in Command and M.O. will inspect billets at 10 a.m.

14. Acknowledge.

25/11/17.

(Signed) G.McDougall, Capt.& Adjt.
2/8th Bn.Manchester Regt.

Issued at 5 p.m.

DISTRIBUTION.
Copy No 1.   199th Inf. Bde.
  "   " 2.   Commanding Officer.
  "   " 3.   2nd in Command.
  "   " 4.   O.C. "A" Coy.
  "   " 5.   "   "B" "
  "   " 6.   "   "C" "
  "   " 7.   "   "D" "
  "   " 8.   "   H.Q. "
  "   " 9.   Q.M.
  "   " 10.   T.O.
  "   " 11.   M.O.
  "   " 12.   R.S.M.
  "   " 13/15 War Diary.
  "   " 16   Spare.

APPENDIX A. 9

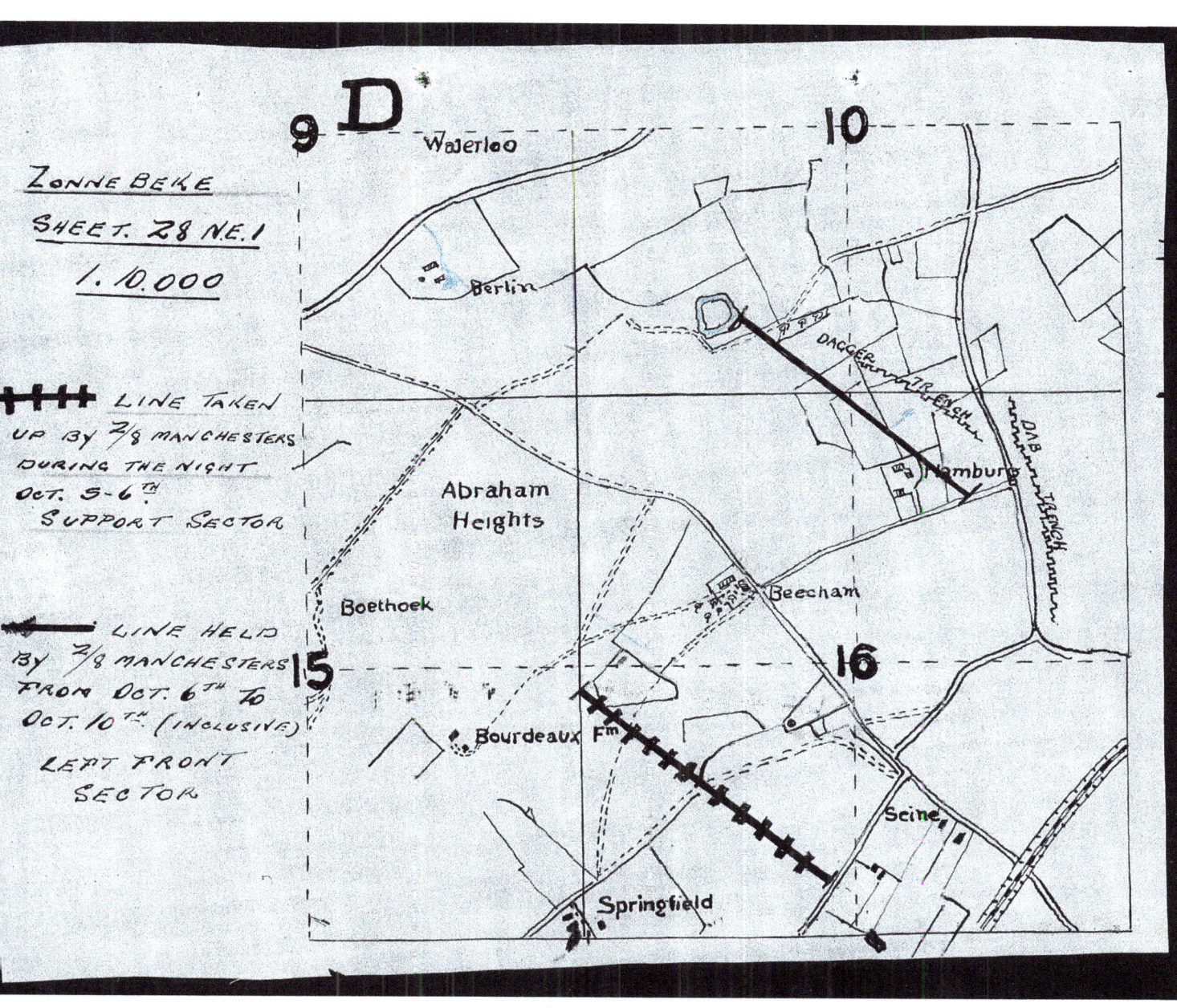

ZONNEBEKE
SHEET. 28 N.E.1
1:10,000

┼┼┼┼ LINE TAKEN UP BY 7/8 MANCHESTERS DURING THE NIGHT OCT. 5-6TH SUPPORT SECTOR

▬▬▬ LINE HELD BY 7/8 MANCHESTERS FROM OCT. 6TH TO OCT. 10TH (INCLUSIVE) LEFT FRONT SECTOR

2/8th Bn. MANCHESTER REGIMENT

WAR DIARY

DECEMBER 1917

Army Form C. 2118.

WAR DIARY
or
INTELLIGENCE SUMMARY.
(Erase heading not required.)

Instructions regarding War Diaries and Intelligence Summaries are contained in F.S. Regs., Part II and the Staff Manual respectively. Title pages will be prepared in manuscript.

Hour, Date, Place	Summary of Events and Information	Remarks and references to Appendices
December 1st 1917 CAESTRE	Company and Specialist Training	
December 2nd 1917 CAESTRE	Organised Sports. Church Parade	
December 3rd 1917 CAESTRE	Company and Specialist Training Organised Sports	
December 4th 1917 CAESTRE	do. do.	
December 5th 1917 CAESTRE	do. do.	
December 6th 1917 CAESTRE	do. do.	
December 7th 1917 CAESTRE	do. do.	
December 8th 1917 CAESTRE	do. do.	
December 9th 1917 CAESTRE	Church Parade. N.C.O.'s Major. Comdg. 2/8th Bn. Manchester Regt.	

Army Form C. 2118.

WAR DIARY
or
INTELLIGENCE SUMMARY.
(Erase heading not required.)

Instructions regarding War Diaries and Intelligence Summaries are contained in F.S. Regs., Part II. and the Staff Manual respectively. Title pages will be prepared in manuscript.

Hour, Date, Place	Summary of Events and Information	Remarks and references to Appendices
December 10th 1917 CAESTRE	Company and Specialist Training organised Group.	
December 11th 1917 CAESTRE	do	
December 12th 1917 CAESTRE	do	
December 13th 1917 CAESTRE	do	
December 14th 1917 CAESTRE	do	
December 15th 1917 CAESTRE	Battalion Drill. Inspection. Brigade Cross Country run. One casualty (accidental)	
December 16th 1917 CAESTRE	Battalion in bus for MONTREAL Camp. Dec 78. H 19 B.	
December 17/917 MONTREAL Camp	Company and Specialist Training	Appendix 1a M.A.Oldham Major Comdg 2/8th Bn. Manchester Regt.

WAR DIARY
or
INTELLIGENCE SUMMARY

(Erase heading not required.)

Army Form C. 2118.

Hour, Date, Place	Summary of Events and Information	Remarks and references to Appendices
December 18th 1917 MONTREAL CAMP	Batt'n supply 300 men and 4 officers as Company as working party to make Corps Bivouac line. No casualty.	
December 19, 1917 MONTREAL CAMP	Batt'n supply 260 men and 4 officers for Company as working party on Corps Support line.	
December 20, 1917 MONTREAL CAMP	Batt'n supply 200 men and 3 officers for Company as working party on Corps Support line.	
December 21, 1917 MONTREAL CAMP		
December 22, 1917 MONTREAL CAMP	Batt'n supply 280 men and 4 officers for Company as working party on Corps Support line.	
December 23 1917 MONTREAL CAMP	Batt'n supply 300 men and 4 officers for Company as working party on Corps Support line.	
December 24 1917 MONTREAL CAMP		
December 25, 1917 MONTREAL CAMP		M.C.L. Watson Major Comdg 2/8th Bn. Manchester Regt.

Army Form C. 2118.

WAR DIARY
or
INTELLIGENCE SUMMARY

(Erase heading not required.)

Instructions regarding War Diaries and Intelligence Summaries are contained in F.S. Regs., Part II. and the Staff Manual respectively. Title pages will be prepared in manuscript.

Hour, Date, Place	Summary of Events and Information	Remarks and references to Appendices
December 26 1917 MONTREAL CAMP	Batn. supply 360 men and 4 officers per Company as working party on Corps Dugout Line.	
December 27 1917 MONTREAL CAMP	do	
December 28 1917 MONTREAL CAMP	do Lt. Col. Mentiers GCM. command of 198 Bgde relieved Lt.Col. Command of this unit	
December 29 1917 MONTREAL CAMP	do	
December 30 1917 MONTREAL CAMP	do	
December 31 1917 MONTREAL CAMP	Batn. supply 360 men and 3 officers per Co. as working party and take up advance party of 2/8 Lancashire Fusiliers Bn. Embus for CAESTRE at 5 p.m. and occupy billets reached December 16th 1917	Appendix A.2. N.G.L. Nolin, Major Comdg. 2/8th Bn. Manchester Regt.

Vol 10

7/8 Bn Manchester Regt.

— War Diary —

Appendices and Casualty Return
for
December 1917

SECRET.

2/8th Batt. Manchester Regiment.

Order No. 54.

Reference :- Sheets 27 and 28,　　　　　　　Copy No.......
　　　　　　　1/40,000.　　　　　　　　　　　　15/12/17.

1. The Battalion will move by bus to the ReNINGHELST area tomorrow.

2. Place of embusment :- CAËSTRE – CASSEL Rd.; just N. of CAËSTRE Station.

3. Companies will be at place of embusment at 7-45 a.m. facing EAST
　　　　　"HQ"　"A" Coy.　"B" Coy.　"C" Coy.　"D" Coy.
　　Men to be told off in 20's.

4. Rations for the day will be issued to and carried by each man.

5. Blankets, officers' valises and mess baskets will be dumped at Q.M. Stores by 5 a.m. Blankets to be neatly rolled in bundles of 10.

6. Dress - F.S.M.O. soft caps; shrapnel helmets on back of packs or on shoulder.

7. "A", "C", and "D" Coys. will each send a NCO to meet Lieut. Lorenzen at Orderly Room at 6-45 a.m., as Advance Party.

8. Billets, and the ground in the vicinity, to be left scrupulously clean.

9. Transport will proceed independently.
　　Starting time - 8-30 a.m.
　　Starting place - Transport Lines.
　　Transport will move with 200 yards distance between "A" and "B" portions.

10. Acknowledge.

　　　　　　　　　　(Signed) G. McDougall, Capt. & Adjt.
　　　　　　　　　　　　2/8th Batt. Manchester Regiment.

Issued at 7-30 PM.

Copy No. 1.　　198th Infantry Brigade.
"　　"　2.　　Commanding Officer.
"　　"　3.　　2nd in Command.
"　　"　4.　　O.C. "A" Coy.
"　　"　5.　　"　"B"　"
"　　"　6.　　"　"C"　"
"　　"　7.　　"　"D"　"
"　　"　8.　　"　"HQ"　"
"　　"　9.　　Medical Officer.
"　　"　10.　 Transport Officer.
"　　"　11.　 Medical Officer.
"　　"　12.　 R.S.M.
"　　"　13/15 War Diary.
"　　"　16.　 Spare.

Appendix /A

Comdg. 2/8th Bn. Manchester Regt.

SECRET.

2/8th Battalion Manchester Regiment.

Order No. 55.

Ref:- Sheets 27 & 28,   Copy No. ....
1/40,000.   30/12/17.

1. The Battalion will be relieved by the 2/5th Bn. Lancs
   Fusiliers to-morrow, 31st inst., and will embus for
   billets occupied previously at CAESTRE.

2. Place of embusment, H.17.b.5.6.

3. Companies will parade in camp ready for embusment at
   about 4 p.m.

4. Dress - F.S.M.O.; soft caps; two blankets per man to
   be carried; shrapnel helmet on shoulder.

5. Officers' valises, mess baskets, etc. will be dumped
   at Camp Entrance by 1 p.m.

6. Huts, and the ground in the vicinity, to be left scrupulously
   clean.
   2nd in Command and M.O. will inspect the huts and lines
   after Coys. have fallen in.

7. Huts occupied by "A", "B", and "HQ" Coys. will be vacated
   by 2 p.m., and no man will be allowed in this portion
   of the camp after this hour.

8. Arrangements are to be made by Coys. for dixies to be
   carried on the busses.

9. Transport will proceed independently to-day, staging for
   one night at BORSCHEPE West.
     Starting Time   11 a.m.
     Starting Place   Transport Lines.
   Transport will move with 200 yards distance between
   A and B portions.

10. Advance Parties.
    The C.Q.M.S. of each Coy. under Lieut. Chandler will leave
    camp at 11 am to-day and proceed as Advance Party.
    Transport Advance Party under 2nd Lt. Sewell will leave
    camp at 7 am to-day, and will report to Area Commandant
    BORSCHEPE West 2 hours before Transport is due to arrive.

11. Acknowledge.

                              (Signed) A. Shaw, 2nd Lieut.
Issued at 10-30 am.   A/Adjutant.
                              2/8th Battalion Manchester Regiment.

DISTRIBUTION.
Copy No. 1.   199th Inf. Bde.
  "   " 2.   2/5th Bn. Lancs. Fusiliers.
  "   " 3.   Commanding Officer.
  "   " 4.   2nd in Command.
  "   " 5.   O.C. "A" Coy.
  "   " 6.   "   "B" "
  "   " 7.   "   "C" "
  "   " 8.   "   "D" "
  "   " 9.   "   "HQ" "
  "   " 10.   T.O.
  "   " 11.   M.O.
  "   " 12.   Q.M.
  "   " 13.   R.S.M.
  "   " 14/16. War Diary.
  "   " 17.   Spare.

Appendix
2 A.

D.L.C. Watkins Major
Comdg. 2/8th Bn. Manchester Regt.

48th Bn. MANCHESTER REGmt

APPENDICES AND CASUALTY RETURN

FOR

DECEMBER 1917

2/8th Bn. Manchester Regt.

CASUALTIES FOR DECEMBER 1917.

Dec. 1st.........Nil.
" 2nd.........Nil.
" 3rd.........Nil.
" 4th.........Nil.
" 5th.........Nil.
" 6th.........Nil.
" 7th.........Nil.
" 8th.........Nil.
" 9th.........Nil.
" 10th.........Nil.
" 11th.........Nil.
" 12th.........Nil.
" 13th.........Nil.
" 14th.........Nil.
" 15th.........Wounded 1 other rank (accidental).
" 16th.........Nil.
" 17th.........Nil.
" 18th.........Wounded 1 other rank.
" 19th.........Nil.
" 20th.........Nil.
" 21st.........Nil.
" 22nd.........Nil.
" 23rd.........Nil.
" 24th.........Nil.
" 25th.........Nil.
" 26th.........Nil.
" 27th.........Nil.
" 28th.........Nil.
" 29th.........Nil.
" 30th.........Nil.
" 31st.........Nil.

V. Wilkin Major
Comdg 2/8th Bn. Manchester Regt.

Army Form C. 2118.

WAR DIARY
or
INTELLIGENCE SUMMARY.
(Erase heading not required.)

Instructions regarding War Diaries and Intelligence Summaries are contained in F. S. Regs., Part II. and the Staff Manual respectively. Title pages will be prepared in manuscript.

Hour, Date, Place	Summary of Events and Information	Remarks and references to Appendices
	Casualties for month ending December	31st 1917
	Wounded — 2 other ranks	

N.A.W. [signature] Major
Comdg 1/8th Bn. Manchester Regt.

2/8th Manchester Reg't

War Diary

for

January 1918

Army Form C. 2118.

WAR DIARY
or
INTELLIGENCE SUMMARY.
(Erase heading not required.)

Instructions regarding War Diaries and Intelligence Summaries are contained in F.S. Regs., Part II and the Staff Manual respectively. Title pages will be prepared in manuscript.

Hour, Date, Place	Summary of Events and Information	Remarks and references to Appendices
January 1st/1918 CAESTRE	Company and Specialist Training	
January 2nd/1918 CAESTRE	do	
January 3rd/1918 CAESTRE	Company and Specialist training. Inspection of Bayonet fighting and P.T. by an American General accompanied by G.O.C. known as Brigade	
January 4th/1918 CAESTRE	Company and Specialist training	
January 5th/1918 CAESTRE	Bath and Brei. Ht. Inspection to	
January 6th/1918 CAESTRE	Bath also Ratis Clever Parades	

W.V. McN. Maj.
Commanding 2/18th Bn.
Manchester Regiment

WAR DIARY
or
INTELLIGENCE SUMMARY.
(Erase heading not required.)

Army Form C. 2118.

Hour, Date, Place	Summary of Events and Information	Remarks and references to Appendices
January 7th/9/18 CAESTRE	Company and Specialist Training	
January 8th/9/18 CAESTRE	Lt Col Herbert wounds command of the Batt on Brig-Gen Hamm returning to Brigade	
January 9th 1918 CAESTRE	Company and Specialist Training. Major Genl Malcolm D.S.O. (G.O.C Division) visit battalion and inspects companies on Assault course	
January 10th 1918 CAESTRE	Company and Specialist Training. Advance billeting party of 1 officer and 6 OR.s W/o for POTIJZE AREA. Batt: transport move to WIPPENHOEK and billet there the night 10/11th previous to moving to BELGIUM CHATEAU emergency line on 11th	Appendix II

B.V. Elliot
Commanding 2/6th
Manchester Regiment

Army Form C. 2118.

WAR DIARY
or
INTELLIGENCE SUMMARY.
(Erase heading not required.)

Instructions regarding War Diaries and Intelligence Summaries are contained in F.S. Regs., Part II. and the Staff Manual respectively. Title pages will be prepared in manuscript.

Hour, Date, Place	Summary of Events and Information	Remarks and references to Appendices
January 11th 1918 CAESTRE	Bn entrain at CAESTRE at 9 a.m. and marches to BELGIUM BATTERY CORNER and thence to POTIJZE dug-out camp "ARGYLE" in the POTIJZE area.	Appendices I A " I C
January 12th 1918 POTIJZE	Bn relieve the 1/8th West Yorks (49th Division) in MOLENAERELSTHOEK Sectr (right sub sector) 66th Divisional front) J.4 & 80.55. Relief completed by 7.17 p.m. "B" Company right front Company, "A" Company Centre, "C" Co support "D" Company left front Company. 'A' Company Reserve. Patrols sent out and connection obtained with units on flanks. Weather fine. Situation normal. Casualties nil.	Appendix II
January 13th 1918 MOLENAERELSTHOEK J.4 & 80.55 Sheet 28 N.E.I.	A fighting patrol sent out at 10.45 p.m. from D.29. 6.02.83. Nothing to report. Situation normal. Casualties Nil. Weather fine.	

W.M.S.
Commanding 2/8th Bn.
Manchester Regiment.

Army Form C. 2118.

WAR DIARY
or
INTELLIGENCE SUMMARY.
(Erase heading not required.)

Instructions regarding War Diaries and Intelligence Summaries are contained in F.S. Regs., Part II. and the Staff Manual respectively. Title pages will be prepared in manuscript.

Hour, Date, Place	Summary of Events and Information	Remarks and references to Appendices
January 14th/1918 MOLENAERSTHOEK J 14 b. 80. 55.	A Contact Patrol established Communication and held to our right. No enemy seen. Situation normal. Snow fell for about 1½ hours from 4.30 a.m. Casualties. 1 O.R. wounded	Appendix I. " II.
January 15th/1918 MOLENAERSTHOEK J 14 b. 80. 55.	Inter Company Relief. A Coy. Right front Company C Coy. Left front Company D Coy. Support Company B Coy. Reserve Company. Situation normal. Weather wet and windy. Casualties. Nil.	
January 16th/1918 MOLENAERSTHOEK J 14 b. 80. 55.	Listening Post established at PLUMTE FARM D 29 b 60. 30. Nothing to report. Situation normal. Weather wet. Casualties Nil	

M.V. ????
Commanding 18th Bn.
Manchester Regiment

Army Form C. 2118.

WAR DIARY
or
INTELLIGENCE SUMMARY.
(Erase heading not required.)

Instructions regarding War Diaries and Intelligence Summaries are contained in F. S. Regs., Part II. and the Staff Manual respectively. Title pages will be prepared in manuscript.

Hour, Date, Place	Summary of Events and Information	Remarks and references to Appendices
January 17/9/18 MOLENACRELSTHOEK. J.4 & 80.55.	Parade (the officers & other O.R's) went out doing orders store at 11.25 a.m. To many Rev. Bryan Yates in goes Civilian Burial. Rations normal. Weather cloudy and wet. Casualties - Nil.	
January 18/9/18 MOLENACRELSTHOEK J.4 & 80.55	Situation normal. Weather fair. Relieved by 2/7th Manchester Regt. Relief complete by 6.45 p.m. Bn. relieved 2/7 L.F. Bn. Manchester Regt 2 in WEST FARM CAMP (I.10 central) Weather fair. Casualties - Nil.	Appendix II f
January 19/9/18 WEST FARM CAMP I.10 central.	Bn. supply 250 men on working parties. Weather fine. Casualties - Nil.	

W. V. Venter
Lt Col
Commanding 2/8th Bn.
Manchester Regiment

(73989) W4141—463. 400,000. 9/14. H.&J.Ltd. Forms/C. 2118/10.

Army Form C. 2118.

WAR DIARY
or
INTELLIGENCE SUMMARY.
(Erase heading not required.)

Instructions regarding War Diaries and Intelligence Summaries are contained in F. S. Regs., Part II. and the Staff Manual respectively. Title pages will be prepared in manuscript.

Hour, Date, Place	Summary of Events and Information	Remarks and references to Appendices
January 20 1918. WEST FARM CAMP. I 10 central.	B" supply 2030 men as working parties remainder of B" m work in Camp. Weather heavy. Casualties Nil.	
January 21 1918. WEST FARM CAMP. I 10 central	do. do.	
January 22 1918. WEST FARM CAMP. I 10 central	B" supply 730 men as working parties. B" relieved by 3/4 B" East Lancs. Regt (198 Bgde) march to INFANTRY BARRACKS, YPRES. B" is relieved 3/5" B" East Lancs. Reg" (198 Bde) Weather heavy. Casualties Nil.	Appendix I.8
January 23 1918. INFANTRY BARRACKS YPRES.	B" supply 300 men as working parties. 190 men for burial Railage CE. Weather fine. Casualties Nil.	

Commanding 2/8th Bn.
Manchester Regiment.

WAR DIARY
or
INTELLIGENCE SUMMARY

Army Form C. 2118.

(Erase heading not required.)

Hour, Date, Place	Summary of Events and Information	Remarks and references to Appendices
January 24 1918 Infantry Barracks YPRES	Bn supply 800 men as working parties. Personnel dumps & Refuge Cr	
January 25 1918 Infantry Barracks YPRES	do	
January 26 1918 Infantry Barracks YPRES	Bn supply 500 men as working parties to various dumps and Refuge Cr. Comdt of Infantry Barracks at YPRES. Barracks for purpose of training n.c.o's. Question of these field cards during we into tents parade. Brig-Genl Balmoral mentioned Major returned. Capt Roo Parmo an officer from each Co recommended as was no and to take over on 28th	
January 27 1918 Infantry Barracks YPRES	Bn supply working parties to ASTRAL dump. Comdt of Infantry becoming vacant Lt-Col Hulbert having been the Bn to attend an course at Toucault. Major Hunter takes Command of Bn	

N. V. Nº——
Commanding 2/8th Bn.
Manchester Regiment

WAR DIARY or INTELLIGENCE SUMMARY

Army Form C. 2118.

Hour, Date, Place	Summary of Events and Information	Remarks and references to Appendices
January 28th 1918. INFANTRY BARRACKS YPRES.	Battalion relieves 4th Lancashire Fusiliers in the DASH CROSSING sector in the front line (left sub-sector 165th Brigade front). D.17.c.50.90. Relief complete 8.30 PM. "B" Coy right front company. "A" Coy left " " "D" Coy support " "C" " reserve " Weather fine, considerable rain. No toe plans were on foot. Left front Coy.	Appendix I
January 29th 1918. DASH CROSSING. D.17.c.50.90 SHEET 28 NE 1	Weather fine, none this 2 O.Rs wounded. Patrol left "D" Coy front at 8.30 PM and proceeded to TIBER COPSE and laid EASTERN edge of same. D.12.d.3.3. returned to D.18.b.50.90 at 10.15 PM. No enemy seen.	Appendix I

N.W.S.G. Lt/Col Comdg 5th Manchester Regt

WAR DIARY or INTELLIGENCE SUMMARY

Army Form C. 2118.

Hour, Date, Place	Summary of Events and Information	Remarks and references to Appendices
January 29th 1918 contd	Patrol left D18a 9.4 at 10.15 pm to reconnoitre Pill Box D18 b 19 and approaches. Way to ASSYRIA. Very bright moonlight. Pillbox every part & abt D18 b 5.7 with M.G. posts and trenches of mostly road from ridge to S.E. Patrol returned without shot being any enemy contact at 3.25am. IPPs and 5 ORs of wound enemy ambush.	
January 30th 1918 DASH CROSSING D19c 50.90	[illegible entries including] "Death" fire, ambushes NIL. later bringing of Appendix II ... 10.55 PM RIbar. complete. 1 Gurkha Scouts brought in at 6.30 PM Found wandering near D18 a 70.60.	W.Refer N.? Capt ? Manchester Regt

WAR DIARY
or
INTELLIGENCE SUMMARY

Army Form C. 2118.

Hour, Date, Place	Summary of Events and Information	Remarks and references to Appendices
January 30th 1918 cont'd	Patrol left D.18.a.77 at 7.25 PM "Lt Boggs + 4 O.Rs; moved along railway embankment towards enemy trench, and D.18.81.8 party of enemy numbering probably 10 were seen, our patrol withdrew and moved L.E. post at D.18.80.75. Patrol left D.12.C.4.4 at 7.30 PM "Lt Petyt + 4 O.Rs; object: to reconnoitre ground No D.19 & 58 Succeeded to TIBER COPSE D.12.d.3.3 after which patrol was found to be impassable owing to. No enemy encountered. Weather fair but misty; casualties nil.	
January 31st 1918 DASH CROSSING D.17.C.30.90		

W.Webb Maj
2/8th Manchester Regt

REMARKS ON TOUR
12/1/18 — 18/1/18.

This tour was comparatively uneventful apart from the bad climatic conditions of frost, thaw & snow. Observation was generally very difficult on this account. Hostile artillery was fairly active chiefly on the W. side of the BROODSEINDE RIDGE. From patrols it was apparent that the enemy only held forward posts about 500x from our line & these he probably only manned by night.

N. v. Ryan
Major
2/8 B.
Manchester Regt.

1/2/18.

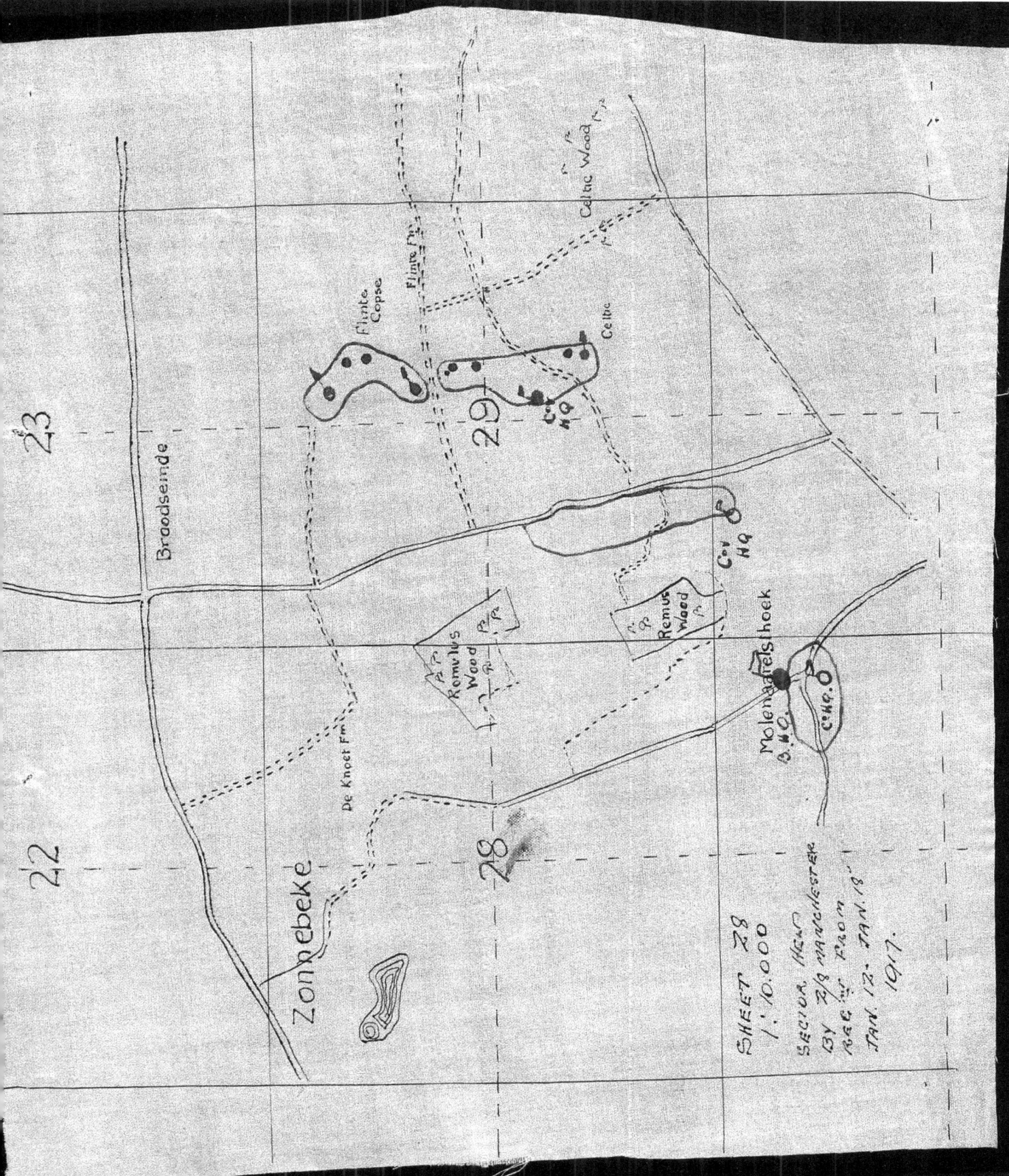

SHEET 28 N.E.I

LEFT FRONT COY with 6 posts   *1 forward L.G. post *.
RIGHT   "   "   *   LISTENING POST by night +
SUPPORT COY   " 2   " LISTENING POST.
RESERVE COY

7/8 Bn MANCHESTER REGmt

CASUALTY RETURN
FOR
JANUARY 1918

Appendix I.

Army Form C. 2118.

WAR DIARY
or
INTELLIGENCE SUMMARY

(Erase heading not required.)

Hour, Date, Place	Summary of Events and Information	Remarks and references to Appendices
	Casualties for month ending January 31st 1918	
	Wounded = 3 O.Rs.	

2/8th Bn. Manchester Regt.

Casualties for month of January 1918.

January 1st 1918..................Nil.
"   2nd   "   ....Nil.
"   3rd   "   ....Nil.
"   4th   "   ....Nil.
"   5th   "   ....Nil.
"   6th   "   ....Nil.
"   7th   "   ....Nil.
"   8th   "   ....Nil.
"   9th   "   ....Nil.
"   10th "   ....Nil.
"   11th "   ....Nil.
"   12th "   ....Nil.
"   13th "   ....Nil.
"   14th "   ....Wounded, other ranks, 1.
"   15th "   ....Nil.
"   16th "   ....Nil.
"   17th "   ....Nil.
"   18th "   ....Nil.
"   19th "   ....Nil.
"   20th "   ....Nil.
"   21st "   ....Nil.
"   22nd "   ....Nil.
"   23rd "   ....Nil.
"   24th "   ....Nil.
"   25th "   ....Nil.
"   26th "   ....Nil.
"   27th "   ....Nil.
"   28th "   ....Nil.
"   29th "   ....Wounded, other ranks, 2.
"   30th "   ....Nil.
"   31st "   ....Nil.

XXX
31/1/18.

Major.
Commanding 2/8th Bn. Manchester Regt.

2/8 Bn. MANCHESTER REGt.

OPERATION ORDERS

FOR

JANUARY 1918

Appendix II.

Secret   APPENDIX "B"   Copy No 8

2/7th Bn. The Manchester Regiment

Operation Order No. 56

1. The Battalion will relieve the 1/4th ROYAL Regiment on the night of the 10th/11th inst.

2. Companies will relieve as follows :-

A Coy will relieve 'X' Coy Reserve Coy
B   "   "   "   'W' " Right Front
C   "   "   "   'Y' " Left   "
D   "   "   "   'Z' " Support Coy

Companies will leave camp in the following order :-

C Coy
B "
D "
A "
Headquarters

2

the leading Company at 1.45 pm, remainder at 15 mins. interval.

3. One guide per platoon and Battalion H.Q. will be at the junction of OXFORD ROAD and ZONNEBEKE ROAD I.5.a.5.8. at 2.0 pm on the 10th inst.

4. Route for ingoing Battalions will be H and K tracks.

5. One guide per advanced post will meet ingoing Units at Company Headquarters at 4.0 pm.

6. In the case of 'W' and 'Y' Companies each guide will be provided with a slip of paper, showing name & number of post, Company and Battalion.

3.

7. Details of work in hand and projected will be handed over together with Secret Maps, aeroplane photographs, Defence Schemes, Reserve Rations, Trench Stores, etc. and signed receipts in duplicate will be forwarded to Battn. H.Q. immediately.

8. Special attention will be paid to taking over Anti-Aircraft Mountings, Food Containers, Water Tins and Trench Stores.

9. Completion of relief will be notified to Battalion H.Q. by wire and Runner by the code word SOCKS.

10. Acknowledge.

9-1-18
Capt.
A/Adjutant
GOAT.

APPENDIX "C"

SECRET   Copy No. 11

2/9th Batt. The Manchester
Regiment

Operation Order No. 55

1. The Battalion will be relieved in the LEFT Front Sector of the line by the 2/10th. Batt The Manchester Regiment on the night 13th/14th January.

2. On completion of relief the Battalion will move to POTIJZE area and take over the Camp vacated by 2/10.th. Manch. Regt, & become Brigade Reserve.

3. The 2/10th Manchester Regt. will take over the line as under:-

2

Right Front   A Company
Left Front   D Company
Support   C Company
Reserve   B Company

4. One guide per platoon (with written instructions will meet the incoming platoons at the junction of The Mule Track and the ZONNEBEKE-FREZENBERG Road (D.26.6.90.40) Guides will report there at 3.30 pm on the 13th inst. 2 Guides will be sent for Battalion H.Q. to report at same place and time. One guide per post of the Front line Companies will meet the incoming Unit at the respective Front line Company H.Q. at 5.30 pm.

5. Defence schemes, maps, Trench Stores & work policy will be carefully handed over & signed receipts

3

5. obtained copies to be forwarded to Battn. H.Q. by 9.0 am on the 14th January.

6. Lewis Gun Limbers will be at FROST HOUSE D.25.c.60.80 at 7.30 pm. on 13th January.

7. Capt. Jill will report to O.C. 2/10th Manch Rgt on the 13th inst. to take over camp.

8. Completion of relief will be reported to Battn. H.Q. by the CODE word "FLY" by wire & runner.

9. Acknowledge

ABmeBapshaw
Capt & Adjt
2/9th Bn. The Manchester Rgt

Copies:—
No 1 198th. Inf. Bde
   2 O.C. 2/10th. Manch R.
   3 2/5th. E. Lancs R.
   4 O.C. A Company
   5 O.C. B Company
   6 O.C. C Company
   7 O.C. D Company
   8 Transport Officer
   9 O.C. Details
  10 File
  11 War Diary

4.

Copies No 1 :- 198th Infantry Brigade
       2 :- 1/4th K.O.Y.L.I. Regt.
       3 :- Commanding Officer.
       4 :- OC A Company
       5 :- OC B Company
       6 :- OC C Company
       7 :- OC D Company
       8 :- War Diary.

SECRET.

2/8th Bn. Manchester Regt.
Order No. 56.

Ref - Sheets 27 and 28.   9/1/18.
      1/40,000.   Copy No.........

1. The Transport will move to-morrow to Transport Lines
   146th Brigade, staging at WIPPENHOEK on the night of the
   10/11th January.

2. Route - CAESTRE - GODEWAERSWELDE - ABEELE - WIPPENHOEK -
           BELGIAN CHATEAU AREA.

3. Starting Point - Bn.H.Q.
   Starting Time - 8 a.m.

4. Mounted advance party will report three hours before arrival
   of Transport at WIPPENHOEK to Lt.Col.MULLINER, Area
   Commandant, WIPPENHOEK.

5. Travelling Kitchens, L.G.Limbers and water carts will be
   detached en route on the 11th inst., and proceed under an
   officer to POTIJZE AREA.
   A guide will report to the Transport Officer at WIPPENHOEK
   on the night of the 10th inst.
   Cooks will arrange for dinners to be ready by 1 am on the
   11th inst.

6. Transport Personnel will take two days rations.

7. Dress - F.S.M.O. with shrapnel helmets and box respirators.

8. Acknowledge.

                              (Sgd) G.McDougall, Capt.& Adjt.
                                 2/8th Bn.Manchester Regiment.
Issued at 6 p.m.
  DISTRIBUTION.
Copy No.1...... 199th Inf.Bde.
 "   " 2...... C.O.
 "   " 3...... 2nd in Command.
 "   " 4...... Transport Officer.
 "   " 5...... Quartermaster.
 "   " 6/8.... War Diary.
 "   " 9...... Spare.

SECRET.   2/8th Bn. Manchester Regiment.
                                Order No. 57.   10/1/18.   13
Reference :- Sheets 27 & 28.   Copy No. 1
               1/40,000.

1. The Brigade will move by bus from CAESTRE to the POTIJZE AREA
   to-morrow. See attached movement table.

2. Starting Point. The Battalion will pass Battalion HQ. at
   8-35 am. in the following order -
        "HQ" Coy. "A" Coy. "C" Coy. "D" Coy. "B" Coy.

3. Details left behind. Details of personnel to be left at
   Transport Lines will follow.

4. Dress. F.S.M.O., shrapnel helmets, and leather jerkins.
   Each man will carry two blankets.

5. R.E. Material. Before leaving areas, Coys. will collect and store
   all loose material, and place near billets or cookhouses.

6. All billets and land in the vicinity of billets will be left
   scrupulously clean.

7. Camp Kettles. All camp kettles, etc. used by Coys. from Jany. 10th-11th
   will be carried by Coys. to the POTIJZE area.
   One camp kettle per platoon will be taken by Coys. into the line.

8. Motor Lorries. Motor Lorries will report at Brigade Office,
   CAESTRE, at 6-45 am.
   The Quartermaster will detail a guide to be at Staff Captain's
   Office at 6-45 am, to conduct the lorry to Q.M. Stores.

9. Guide. A guide from billeting party will report to Quartermaster
   to-night to conduct lorries to Q.M. Stores, BELGIAN CHATEAU, on the
   11th inst.

10. Baggage. Officers' valises, and all Coy. Stores will be
    delivered to Q.M. Stores by 6 am. 11th. As much as possible should
    be delivered by 6 pm. to-night.

11. Area Stores. All area stores on charge of units in back area
    will be collected together prior to departure, and handed over
    to Area Commandant, from whom receipts will be obtained.
    The 2nd in Command is responsible that this is done, and will
    forward copies of receipts to Brigade Headquarters by 12th inst.

12. Trench Foot Powder. Trench Foot Powder will be drawn from
    Brigade Q.M. Stores on 12th inst. and distributed to Coys.
    The 2nd in Command is responsible that this is done.

13. Rations. Rations for consumption on 12th will be delivered
    on the 11th by Transport to POTIJZE AREA.
    Rations for consumption on the 12th., and until further notice,
    will be drawn by 1st line transport.

14. Runners. On the 11th, on arrival at Transport Lines, the
    Quartermaster will detail two runners to report to Staff Captain,
    Brigade Rear Headquarters, Infantry Barracks, YPRES. They will
    have the unexpired portion of days rations. From the 12th
    onwards they will be rationed by Brigade.

15. Trench Orders. The attention of Company Commanders is drawn
    to 66th Division Trench Orders, already issued.

16. Acknowledge.
                        (Signed) G. McDougall, Capt. & Adjt.
                                2/8th Bn. Manchester Regiment.
Issued at 10-30 pm.
                                                            B.T.O.

DISTRIBUTION.

Copy No.1....149th Infantry Brigade.
"   " 2....Commanding Officer.
"   " 3....2nd in Command.
"   " 4....O.C. "A" Coy.
"   " 5.... "   "B" "
"   " 6.... "   "C" "
"   " 7.... "   "D" "
"   " 8.... "   "HQ" "
"   " 9....Q.M.
"   "10....M.O.
"   "11....R.S.M.
"   "12/14.War Diary.
"   "15....Spare.

Date   MOVEMENT TABLE - 199TH INFANTRY BRIGADE.
Jan.11th 1918.

Unit in order of embussing.	Embussing Point.	Times ready to embus.	Column moves.	Debussing Point.	Destination.	No.of busses.	Remarks.
304 M.G.C.	) CAESTRE -) ST.SYLVESTRE) CAPPEL Road) Column) facing E.) Head at) Q.21.b.x.4.	8-45am.	9-30am.	WARATAH CAMP G.15.c.29	WARATAH CAMP	1 - 7	C.Os. will detail guides from the advance parties to meet units at debussing points at 10-30am & guide them to their billeting area.
199th L.T.M.B.		8-45 am.	9-3 am.	) Road N.) of KRUIS-) TRAAT) From) H.18.a.90) to) H.19.d.46	(POTIJZE AREA.)	8 - 10	
2/6th M/sters		9 am.	"			11 - 37	
2/7th "		"	"			38 - 61	
2/8th "		8-45am.	"			62 - 91	
2/5th "		9 am.	"			92 - 121	
Bde.HQ.		"	"			122 - 126	
2/3rd Fld. Ambulance. (dismounted portion)	Rue d'Eglise HAZEBROUCK.	8-30 am.	9 am.	WARATAH CAMP G.15.c.29.	WARATAH CAMP.	Six.	

SECRET.

2/8th Bn. Manchester Regt.
Order No.68.

Reference :- Sheets 27 & 28.
1/10,000.

10/1/18.
Copy No. 12

1. R.E.PLATOON.
   On arrival at POTIJZE area, each Coy. will detail one section of one NCO and six men from one platoon to report at Battalion Headquarters. These men will take full kit, and rations up to evening of 13th inst.
   2nd Lt. Robson will be in charge of this platoon, and will report with the platoon to Capt. Phethean, of the 2/5th Manch.Regt. at time and place to be notified later.

2. MEN FOR Y.M.C.A.
   Men detailed for the above will report to Battalion H.Q. POTIJZE at 2-30 on the 11th, and will receive orders.
   They will be provided with three days rations.

3. BRIGADE SIGNALLING CLASS.
   All men attending recent course at Brigade Signalling Class, and ten other ranks to be detailed by O.C. "HQ" Coy. will march from the place of debussing to the Transport Lines.

4. PIONEERS.
   Pioneers, less two detailed by O.C. "HQ" Coy. to go up the line, will proceed from debussing point to Transport Lines.

5. 2nd Lt. Baggs will take charge of all men proceeding from debussing point to transport lines, and remaining there.

6. Any other men not proceeding to the trenches will be sent back from POTIJZE.

                            (Signed) G. McDougall, Capt.& Adjt.
Issued at 3 pm.   2/8th Bn. Manchester Regiment.

DISTRIBUTION.
Copy No. 1.   199th Infantry Brigade.
  "   " 2.   Commanding Officer.
  "   " 3.   2nd in Command.
  "   " 4.   O.C. "A" Coy.
  "   " 5.   " "B" "
  "   " 6.   " "C" "
  "   " 7.   " "D" "
  "   " 8.   " "HQ" "
  "   " 9.   Q.M.
  "   " 10.   M.O.
  "   " 11.   R.S.M.
  "   " 13/14. War Diary.
  "   " 15.   Spare.

SECRET.
2/8th Battalion Manchester Regt.
Order No. 59.

Ref:- Sheet 28.
1/40,000.

12/1/18.

Copy No............

1. The Battalion will relieve the 1/8th Bn. West Yorks Regt. on January 13th 1918.

2. Right Front Coy..........."D" Coy.
   Left   do.   ...."B" Coy.
   Support Coy   ...."C" Coy.
   Reserve Coy. ...."A" Coy.

3. Order of March.
   "B" Coy. "D" Coy. "C" Coy. "A" Coy. "HQ" Coy.

4. Distance. - 200 yards between platoons.

5. Guides. (1 per platoon) will meet leading platoons at junction of BOLF TRACK and CAMBRIDGE ROAD, I.11.b.1.2. at 1 pm.

6. Dress - Greatcoats to be worn, and packs.

7. Exact details of strengths of Coys. will be given verbally to Coy. Commanders to-morrow.

8. Blankets, neatly rolled in bundles of 10, Haversacks, and P.H.Helmets, to be dumped at Orderly Room to-morrow morning.
   Blankets by 9 a.m.
   Haversacks and P.H.Helmets, by 11 a.m.

9. Stores, etc.
   All reserve supplies, ammunition, trench and area stores, and documents, will be carefully checked before being taken over, and receipts will be given.
   Copies of all receipts will be forwarded to Bn. H.Q. on the 17th inst.

10. Solidified Alcohol.- will be issued to Coys. with Saturday's rations.

11. Trench Feet.
    (1) Attention is drawn to Divisional letter 2431/A dated 13/12/17, which is in possession of all officers. Every man's feet are to be carefully washed and treated as laid down in the above letter before going into the trenches.
    (2) Every man going into the trenches must be in possession of two pairs of socks, in addition to those he is wearing.
    (3) Every day the socks of all men in the line will be changed, the discarded socks being put into sandbags - one sandbag per platoon. Sandbags to be labelled with the Company and Platoon, and sent by rations carriers to Battalion H.Q. Clean socks will be delivered each night.

12. Personnel of front line Coys. will not be sent back under any consideration whatever, with the exception of Coy. Runners and Stretcher Bearers.

13. The extreme importance of the position which the Battalion is about to take over, and the necessity for the most vigorous action in the event of a temporary hostile success, must be impressed on all ranks. The whole of the front line system is to be held at all costs. If the enemy does succeed in penetrating into any part of our position, he is to be ejected at once by immediate local counter-attack.

14. One Officer per front line Coy. and one officer from Battalion H.Q. will be left behind by the outgoing Battalion for 24 hours.

P.T.O.

15. Completion of relief to be reported in writing by codeword "READY"

16. Acknowledge.

(Sgd) G. McDougall, Capt.& Adjt.
Issued at 7 pm.   1/5th Bn. Manchester Regiment.

DISTRIBUTION.

Copy No. 1. 165th Infantry Brigade.
"   " 2. Commanding Officer.
"   " 3. 2nd in Command.
"   " 4. O.C. "A" Coy.
"   " 5.   "   "B" "
"   " 6.   "   "C" "
"   " 7.   "   "D" "
"   " 8.   "   "HQ" "
"   " 9. M.O.
"   " 10. T.O.
"   " 11. Q.M.
"   " 12. R.S.M.
"   " 13/15. War Diary.
"   " 16. Spare.

SECRET.

2/8th Bn. Manchester Regiment.
Order No. 60.

Reference :- Sheet No. 28.
1/40,000.

14/1/18.
Copy No........

1. Relief of Front Line Companies will take place to-morrow evening, 15th inst., as follows:-
   "A" Coy. will relieve "B" Coy. in Right Front Line.
   "C" Coy. will relieve "D" Coy. in Left Front Line.

2. On relief "D" Coy. will occupy SUPPORT line vacated by "C" Coy.
   "B" Coy. will occupy RESERVE position vacated by "A" Coy.

3. Guides (1 per post and 1 for Coy. HQ) of Front Line Coy. will meet relieving companies at forward end of their respective communication trenches at
   "B" Coy. at 5 p.m.
   "D" Coy. at 6 p.m.
   Relieving Coys. will detail the garrison for each post before moving, and garrisons of posts will move separately at intervals of 5 minutes.

4. Relieving Coys. will have guides at the rear end of the respective Communication Trenches to meet the relieved Companies.
   "A" Coy. will leave 4 guides, who after guiding the outcoming Coy. to the Reserve Dugouts, will guide the ration parties to be found by "B" Coy. to the ration dump, and will afterwards guide the meal carrying parties of "B" Coy. to the Front Line Companies.
   "C" Coy. will leave a guide for each SUPPORT post.
   O.C. "D" Coy. will detail garrisons for the SUPPORT posts before leaving the Front Line.

5. All trench stores, maps, defence schemes, etc. will be carefully handed and taken over, and receipts given. Copies of receipts will be sent in to Battalion H.Q. on 15th inst.

6. All posts, dugouts, etc. are to be left scrupulously clean.

7. Completion of relief will be reported to Battalion H.Q. by code word "DONE".

8. Work. Os.C. "A" and "C" Coys. will hand over to Os.C. "B" and "D" Coys. respectively exact details of work done by Support and Reserve Coys., giving description of work, number of men on each task, hours worked.

9. Acknowledge.

(Sgd) G. McDougall, Capt. & Adjt.
2/8th Bn. Manchester Regiment.

Issued at 7 p.m.

DISTRIBUTION.
Copy No. 1......199th Infty. Bde.
"   "   2......Commanding Officer.
"   "   3......2nd in Command.
"   "   4......O.C. "A" Coy.
"   "   5...... "   "B" "
"   "   6...... "   "C" "
"   "   7...... "   "D" "
"   "   8...... "   "HQ" "
"   "   9......M.O.
"   " 10......T.O.
"   " 11......Q.M.
"   " 12......R.S.M.
"   " 13/15...War Diary.
"   " 16......Spare.

SECRET.
                    2/8th Bn. Manchester Regiment.
                         Order No. 61.
Reference :- Sheet No. 28.   17/1/18.
            1/40,000.   Copy No........

1. The Battalion will be relieved to-morrow by 2/7th Bn.
   Manchester Regiment.

2. Guides will be found by "B" and "D" Coys. as follows :-
     By "D" Coy. 1 other rank per post and 1 other rank
     for "HQ" (Total 4 other ranks) for Support Coy.
     By "B" Coy. 1 other rank per pill-box and 1 other rank
     for HQ (Total 4 other ranks) for Reserve Coy.
     By HQ. Coy. One other rank for Bn. H.Q.
   These guides to be at junction of MOLE TRACK and CAMBRIDGE
   ROAD (I.11.b.1.7.) at 1 p.m.

     By "B" Coy. 1 officer and 4 other rank per post (Total
     5 other ranks) for Right Front Line Coy.
     By "D" Coy. 1 officer and 4 other rank per post (Total
     4 other ranks) for Left Front Line Coy.
   These guides to be at junction of MOLE TRACK and CAMBRIDGE
   ROAD (I.11.b.1.7.) at 2 p.m.

3. All trench stores, defence schemes, maps, etc. will be
   handed over, and receipts taken. Copies of receipts will
   be rendered to Battalion H.Q. by noon on 19th inst.
     Note. - Lewis Gun Magazines, Camp Kettles, Dixies, and
   Gum Boots will not be handed over, but will be taken
   out. On arrival in camp gum boots will be immediately
   collected for drying with the tops turned down.

4. All posts, dugouts, latrines, etc. must be left scrupulously
   clean.

5. March discipline must be strictly maintained on the way
   out. An officer or N.C.O. will march in rear of each party,
   and will be responsible that there is no straggling.

6. On completion of relief Coys. will move independently
   via MOLE TRACK to hutted CAMP at I.10.Central.

7. The Quartermaster will arrange to have the quarters for
   each Company in Camp allotted before arrival of the Battalion.
   He will have a hot meal ready, and arrange for transport
   of blankets and officers' valises to the Camp.

8. Completion of relief will be immediately reported to
   Battalion H.Q. by wire, using code word "GLAD".

9. Acknowledge.

                           (Sgd) G. McDougall, Capt. & Adjt.
                           2/8th Bn. Manchester Regiment.

Issued at 4-30 pm.
DISTRIBUTION.
Copy No. 1. 199th Infty. Bde.
  "   " 2. 2/7th Manchester R.
  "   " 3. Commanding Officer.
  "   " 4. 2nd in Command.
  "   " 5. O.C. "A" Coy.
  "   " 6. "   "B" "
  "   " 7. "   "C" "
  "   " 8. "   "D" "
  "   " 9. "   "HQ" "
  "   "10. M.O.
  "   "11. T.O.
  "   "12. Q.M.
  "   "13. R.S.M.
  "   "14/16. War Diary.
  "   "17. Spare.

SECRET.

2/8th Bn. Manchester Regiment.
Order No. 62.

Ref :- Sheet No. 28.
1/40,000.

Copy No. ...17....
21/1/18.

1. The Battalion will proceed to YPRES BARRACKS to-morrow.

2. Route - MENIN ROAD - MENIN GATE - BARRACKS.

3. Order of March - "HQ" Coy., "A" Coy., "C" Coy., "B" Coy., "D" Coy.

4. Starting Time - "HQ" Coy. "A" Coy. and "C" Coy. - 3-15 pm.
   "B" Coy. and "D" Coy. - 4-30 pm.

5. Platoons at 200 yards distance.

6. Dress - F.S.M.O., shrapnel helmets; gas box respirators at the "alert".

7. The strictest march discipline will be observed.
   Platoon Sergts. will march in front of their platoons.
   Platoon Commanders will march in rear of their platoons.

8. Six huts, to be indicated by 2nd Lt. Shaw, will be vacated by 9-30 am, to allow the incoming unit to occupy them.

9. All huts, cookhouses, latrines, and lines will be left scrupulously clean.

10. The 2nd in Command and the Medical Officer will inspect the Camp when the huts are vacated.

11. Blankets will be neatly rolled, and labelled, in bundles of ten, and will be ready for loading at 9-30 am.
    Officers' valises and all stores will be ready at 11-30 am.
    Baggage wagons will report at 10 am.

12. Lewis gun limbers will report at 9 am. Coys. will load them at once.

13. Travelling kitchens and water carts will be ready to move at 4 p.m. Coys. will make arrangements to have tea ready on arrival.

14. Acknowledge.

(Sgd) G. McDougall, Capt. & Adjt.
Issued at 9 pm.   2/8th Bn. Manchester Regiment.
DISTRIBUTION.
Copy No. 1....199th Bde.
  "   " 2....2/4th East Lancs. Regt.
  "   " 3....2/5th East Lancs. Regt.
  "   " 4....Commanding Officer.
  "   " 5....2nd in Command.
  "   " 6....O.C. "A" Coy.
  "   " 7.... " "B" "
  "   " 8.... " "C" "
  "   " 9.... " "D" "
  "   " 10.... " "HQ" "
  "   " 11.... M.O.
  "   " 12.... T.O.
  "   " 13.... Q.M.
  "   " 14.... R.S.M.
  "   " 15/17.. War Diary.
  "   " 18.... Spare.

SECRET.

2/6th Bn. Manchester Regt.
Order No. 91.

Reference to Sheet No. 28.   22/1/18.
1/40,000.   Copy No............

1. The Battalion will relieve the 2/8th Bn. Lancashire
   Fusiliers to-day.

2. Right Front Coy.   - "B" Coy.
   Left Front Coy.   - "D" Coy.
   Support Coy.   - "A" Coy.
   Reserve Coy.   - "C" Coy.

3. Starting Times.
   "A" Coy, "C" Coy, and "H.Q" Coy. - 1-30 p.m.
   "B" and "D" Coys. - 2-30 p.m.

4. Distances.   200 yards between platoons.

5. Guides.
   (a) One per Batt. H.Q., Reserve Coy., and Support Coy.
   (b) One per post Front Line.
   meet at (a) 2-30 p.m. FRONT HOUSE. (b) 3-30 p.m. FRONT HOUSE.

6. Route.   Mule Track alongside of Rly. "E" track. If tracks
   are being heavily shelled, Os.C.Coys. may use their
   discretion by using other tracks.

7. Dress - Trench Fighting Order, greatcoats neatly rolled,
   groundsheets under the flap of the haversack, water bottles
   filled.

8. Coys. will take over posts, etc. from the Coys. which they
   are relieving as at present held.

9. Blankets to be neatly rolled in bundles of 10, will be
   dumped at entrance of barracks by 9-30 a.m.
   Officers' vallises, packs, and P.H.Helmets at entrance of
   barracks by 10-30 a.m.

10. All reserve supplies of ammunition, trench stores,
    documents, etc., will be carefully checked before being
    taken over, and receipts given. Copies of all receipts
    to be forwarded to Battalion H.Q. by 9 a.m. on the
    24th inst.

11. Trench Feet.   Particular attention is drawn to Divisional
    letter 2471/A dated 19/12/17. All officers will make
    themselves thoroughly acquainted with the contents of this
    letter, and will ensure that all ranks are thoroughly
    acquainted with the procedure laid down therein, which
    is to be strictly complied with.
    The Medical Officer will supervise the final treatment
    before going into the line, and will render a certificate
    that this has been properly carried out by 1 p.m. to-day.
    He will be responsible that the correct amount of powder
    is issued to Coys. during the tour.

12. Socks.   Coy. Commanders will render a certificate by 12 noon
    that all men in their Coy. are in possession of three pairs
    of socks, and a certificate will be rendered daily by all
    Coys. in the line that the treatment as laid down in
    Divisional letter 2471/A has been carried out.

13. The importance of positions which the Battalion is taking
    over should be impressed on all ranks, and the whole of
    the front line system is to be held at all costs. In the
    event of the enemy penetrating any part of the line, he
    is to be immediately ejected by counter-attack without
    further orders.

(1).

14. One limber is allotted between "A" and "B" Coys. and one between "C" and "D" Coys. for Lewis guns and ammunition. These limbers will be loaded at the Barracks by 1 p.m., and will proceed to FROST HOUSE, where the Coys. will pick up their respective guns and ammunition. One N.C.O. and one man per Coy. will accompany this limber.

15. Coys. will arrange with 2nd Lt. Shaw to draw one pair of gumboots for each man going into the line before noon to-day from the Brigade Gum Boot Store at Infantry Barracks.

16. Completion of relief will be reported by code-word "SOCKS".

17. All the barrack rooms must be thoroughly cleaned out by 1-15 p.m. 2nd Lt. Shaw and the Medical Officer will inspect all billets at 1-30 p.m.

18. Acknowledge.

(Signed) G. McDougall, Capt. & Adjt.
9/8th Bn. Manchester Regiment.

<u>Issued at 8-15 a.m.</u>

DISTRIBUTION.
Copy No. 1.......126th Inf. Bde.
" " 2.......9/8th Bn. Lancs. Fusiliers.
" " 3.......Commanding Officer.
" " 4.......2nd in Command.
" " 5.......O.C. "A" Coy.
" " 6....... " "B" "
" " 7....... " "C" "
" " 8....... " "D" "
" " 9....... " "HQ" "
" " 10......M.O.
" " 11......T.O.
" " 12......Q.M.
" " 13......R.S.M.
" " 14/15...War Diary.
" " 17.   Spare.

War Diary 2/8th Manc R.

for

Oct 1918

Vol. 12.

WAR DIARY
or
INTELLIGENCE SUMMARY

(Erase heading not required.)

Army Form C. 2118.

Instructions regarding War Diaries and Intelligence Summaries are contained in F. S. Regs., Part II. and the Staff Manual respectively. Title pages will be prepared in manuscript.

Hour, Date, Place	Summary of Events and Information	Remarks and references to Appendices
Feb 1st Left Sub Sector. 66th Divisional Front.	Weather fine but windy. Casualties Nil. Listening patrols observed enemy working party at PIL BOX D.18.a.70.93. Artillery shoot party dispersed with casualties. Two stretcher cases + one sarcentures.	
Feb 2nd do	Weather fine. Casualties Nil. Patrol of 1NCO+4OR' wire CE left D19 a.6.3 & went due E 250yds up position in shell hole + swept right & roundabout 400° E with short dusk. Movement had been seen there at 6 a.m. in morning	
Feb 3rd 20 16 ANZAC Support Battn Left Sub. 66th Divisional Front.	Weather fine. Casualties Nil. 9/7th Manchesters left relieved Battn. Relief complete 5.30 pm. Battn took over position vacated by 9/7 Manch Regt as Support Battn Left Brigade. "D" Coy DARING CROSSING D16.a.70.30 attached 9/7 Manchester Regt for tactical purposes + working parties.	appendices II a

WAR DIARY
or
INTELLIGENCE SUMMARY.
(Erase heading not required.)

Army Form C. 2118.

Hour, Date, Place	Summary of Events and Information	Remarks and references to Appendices
Feb 3rd 1917	A Coy. THAMES D22 to 30.30 attached to 176 Tunnel Regt for tactical purposes & working parties. C Coy ALBANIA J3 b 30.90. Working party of 1 Officer 2 Sjts + 50 O.R" supplied daily to R.E° for work on road repairing at ZONNEBEKE. B Coy ANZAC J3 a 10.40 Working party of 1 Officer + Sjt 50 O.R° supplied to R.E° daily for road repairing at ZONNEBEKE. Battn H Q ANZAC HOUSE J3 a 20.40.	
Feb 4th do	Weather fine. Casualties NIL.	
Feb 5th do	Weather fine. Casualties NIL. Lt Col Heathcot returns from conference & reconnaissance at transport lines, BELGIAN BATTERY CORNER.	

WAR DIARY
or
INTELLIGENCE SUMMARY.
(Erase heading not required.)

Army Form C. 2118.

Instructions regarding War Diaries and Intelligence Summaries are contained in F.S. Regs., Part II and the Staff Manual respectively. Title pages will be prepared in manuscript.

Hour, Date, Place	Summary of Events and Information	Remarks and references to Appendices
Feb 6th do	Weather fair, Casualties Nil.	
Feb 7th do	Weather wet Casualties Nil.	
Feb 8th do	Weather wet. Casualties Nil.	
Feb 9th do RENINGHELST AREA	Weather fair. Casualties Nil. Battalion moved to RENINGHELST AREA, HQ, B & C Coys moved without relief at 3 pm. A Coy moved out 5.15 pm D " " 5.30 pm	Appendix II
Feb 10th do	Weather. Casualties wounded 1 OR accidental. Details who were not in line joined Batt.	
Feb 11th do SCHOOL CAMP (Sheet 27 L.3.d)	Batt" moved to SCHOOL CAMP (Sheet 27 L.3.d) starting time 7am. Weather fair Casualties Nil.	Appendix II C

WAR DIARY or INTELLIGENCE SUMMARY

Army Form C. 2118.

Hour, Date, Place	Summary of Events and Information	Remarks and references to Appendices
Feb 12th Do	Weather fair. Casualties Nil. Battalion paraded for inspection by GOC Division.	
Feb 13th Do	Weather wet. Casualties Nil. Batt'n disbanded as follows:- 10 Officers 188 OR° to 9/5 Manchester Regt. 11 Officers 197 OR° to 9/6 " 10 Officers 209 OR° to 9/7 " 3 Officers 35 OR° to BERTHEN 22nd Corps 1 Officer 36 OR° Transport to 199th Inf. Brigade. Lt Col Hurlbut proc'd to command 6th the Bn the R.I.R. Lares two. All stores etc returned to armuries. WAR DIARY CLOSED 13th Feb 1918	Hurlbut Lt Col Comm'g 9th Bn R. Ir. R.

Army Form C. 2118.

WAR DIARY
or
INTELLIGENCE SUMMARY.
(Erase heading not required.)

Instructions regarding War Diaries and Intelligence Summaries are contained in F.S. Regs., Part II. and the Staff Manual respectively. Title pages will be prepared in manuscript.

Hour, Date, Place	Summary of Events and Information	Remarks and references to Appendices
	Casualties for Feb ending 13th wounded 3 O.R.	

2/8 Batt'n Manchester Reg't

CASUALTY RETURN

FOR

Feb 1918

appendix I

2/8th. Battalion Manchester Regt.

CASUALTIES.

1/2/18................Wounded. O.R.....1.
2/2/18................   N I L.
3/2/18................   N I L.
4/2/18................   N I L.
5/2/18................   N I L.
6/2/18................   N I L.
7/2/18................   N I L.
8/2/18................   N I L.
9/2/18................   N I L.
10/2/18...............Wounded (Accidental.) O.R....1.
11/2/18...............   N I L.
12/2/18...............   N I L.
13/2/18...............   N I L.

14/2/18.

G. MacDougall
Captain Adjt
for Lieut. Colonel.
Commanding 2/8th. Battalion Manchester Regt.

2/6 Batt'n Manchester Reg't

"OPERATION ORDERS"

for

Feb 1918

Appendix II

1/8th. Battalion Manchester Regiment.
Order No. 43.

Ref. - Sheet No. 28.   Copy No.........
      1/40,000.   8/7/18.

1. The Battalion will move to REMINGHELST Area on the evening
   of the 9th.

2. Headquarters and "B" and "C" Coys. will move to POTIJZE without
   relief at 5.p.m.
   "A" Coy. will move to POTIJZE at 5-15.p.m.
   "D" Coy will move to POTIJZE at 5-30.p.m.
   All movements East of FRESHWATER RIVER will be by sections.
   Units may use ZONNEBEKE ROAD.
   The Battalion will entrain at POTIJZE (det ils to follow).

3. L.G.Limbers will be at Ration Dump ANZAC HOUSE at 5.p.m.
   for "B" and "C" Coys., who will arrange to load at that time.
   L.G.Limbers will meet "A" and "D" Coys., in the POTIJZE -
   ZONNEBEKE ROAD, where the Coys., will load.

4. 2nd. Lt. Tongue will superintend the loading of all Limbers,
   and he will proceed to Details.
   L.G.Limbers will return to Transport Lines directly they are
   loaded.

5. Coys. will march out with -
   (a) All L.G.Magazines full.
   (b) All men with 150 rounds S.A.A.
   A certificate to this effect will be rendered to Battalion
   Headquarters at REMINGHELST on arrival.

6. All lines to be left scrupulously clean, the Medical Officer
   to inspect Battalion H.Q., ALBANIA and ANZAC.

7. All Trench Stores in possession of Coys., will be delivered to
   Battalion H.Q. ANZAC HOUSE by 12 noon 9th. inst.
   The following will be taken out by Coys.-
   (a) Waterproof Ration Bags.
   (b) A.A.Sights for Lewis Guns.
   (c) Dummy S.A.A.

8. Q.M. and T.O. will arrange to carry blankets and Officers' and
   Men's kits to REMINGHELST on the 9th.

9. Q.M. will detail guides for Lorries mentioned in
   Administrative Order No. 77.

10. Q.M.Stores and Transport will move on the 11th.(Details to
    follow.)

11. Lieut. Chandler will proceed from POTIJZE to Details, and with
    three cyclists detailed by O.C. Details, will report to A/Staff
    Captain at 6.a.m. on the 10th at Reserve Bde.H.Q. N.19.b.1.4.
    WINNIPEG CAMP. Rations will be carried for the 11th.

12. Details left out of trenches will rejoin their units on the 10th.

13. Acknowledge.

                                (Signed) S. McDougall, Captain & Adjutant.
                                         1/8th. Battalion Manchester Regt.
Issued at 1a.m.
Copy No. 1. 126th. Inf. Bde.
    "   " 2. C.O.
    "   " 3. 2nd. in Command.   Copy No. 9. O.C. Details.
    "   " 4. O.C."A" Coy.   "   " 10. M.O.
    "   " 5. " "B" "   "   " 11. T.O.
    "   " 6. " "C" "   "   " 12. Q.M.
    "   " 7. " "D" "   "   " 13. R.S.M.
    "   " 8. " "E" "   "   "14/15. War Diary.
                                     "   " 17. Spare.

SECRET.

2/6th. Batt. Manchester Regt.
Order. No. 27.

Ref.   Copy No...........
                                                             10/9/16.

1. The Battalion will proceed to SCHOOL CAMP (Sheet 27 - L.S.d.) tomorrow.

2. Starting point - Level Crossing, RENINGHELST.

3. Starting Time - 7 a.m.

4. Order of March - H.Q., "A" "B" "C" and "D" Coys.
   (Headquarters will form up W. of Crossing.
   All Signallers will march in a formed body in front of the Battalion.)

5. Dress - F.S.M.O., Shrapnel Helmets will be worn.

6. Distances - 100 yards between platoons, and companies.

7. Prescribed halts, will be observed, with the exception of the halt at 9.50.a.m., which will be for 15 minutes (9.50.a.m. to 10.5.a.m.), to allow for correction of any mistakes in intervals.

8. The greatest attention will be paid to -
   (1). Uniformity of turnout, and cleanliness.
   (2). March discipline.

9. Lines will be left scrupulously clean.

10. The Medical Officer will inspect the lines after the Battalion has moved off.

11. Transport will move with the Battalion. Special attention is called to distances between Transport. See Fourth Army No. G.S.148.

12. Order of March of Transport will be as follows :-
    10 Limbers.
    2 Watercarts.
    4 Travelling Kitchens.
    1 Maltese Cart.
    1 Officers' Mess Cart.
    2 Baggage Wagons.

13. When "Marching past", rifles will be slung over right shoulder. Eyes Right (or Left), will be given by Platoon Commanders.

14. Company Commanders will be mounted. Dismounted officers - F.S.M.O.

15. Lurry for conveyance of baggage, will report at 8.a.m.
    The Q.M., will detail a guide for Lurry to report at Staff Captain's Office at 7.45.a.m., and to conduct Lurry to the Battalion at RENINGHELST.
    Lieut. Chandler is detailed to meet the lurries, and superintend the loading.

16. Blankets, neatly rolled in bundles of 10, and officers' kits, and Mess kit, will be dumped at Camp entrance, ready for loading.
    "H.Q" Blankets, and Officers' kits at H.Q.

17. 2nd.Lt. Blackwell and men at Details Camp will form rear party, and be responsible for cleanliness of Detail Camp, Q.M.Stores, Transport Lines. They will then march to RENINGHELST, and report to Lieut. Chandler, under whom they will march to SCHOOL CAMP. The abovementioned Officers will obtain certificates from Area Commandant concerned, that the respective camps, have been left clean.

18. Acknowledge.

                        (Signed) G. McDougall. Captain & Adjutant.
                                 2/6th. Batt. Manchester Regiment.

                                                             P. T. O.

DISTRIBUTION.

Copy No. 1. 108th. Inf. Bde.
"   "   2. C.O.
"   "   3. 2nd. in Command.
"   "   4. O.C. "A" Coy.
"   "   5. "   "B" "
"   "   6. "   "C" "
"   "   7. "   "D" "
"   "   8. "   "HQ" "
"   "   9. T. O.
"   " 10. Q. M.
"   " 11. M. O.
"   " 12. R.S.M.
"   " 13/15. War Diary.
"   " 16. Spare.

SECRET
2/8th Bn Manchester Regiment.   Copy No. 13
               Order No.

Reference Sheet 28
           1/40,000.

1. The Battalion will be relieved tomorrow, Feb. 3rd by
   2/7th Bn Manchester Regiment.

2. Guides as follows will be at Bn. H.Q at 4 p.m. to meet
   relieving Companies:—
         "A" + "C" Coys – 1 Guide per post + 1 guide for Coy H.Q.
         "B" + "D" Coys – 1 Guide per platoon + 1 guide for Coy H.Q.

3. On relief Coys will proceed to positions in Support as
   follows:—
         "A" Coy to THAMES.   D 22 b 5.5.
         "B" Coy to ANZAC.   J 3 a 1.4.
         "C" Coy to ALBANIA. J 3 b 4.8.
         "D" Coy to DARING CROSSING. D 16 d 6.2.
         Battalion H.Q will be at ANZAC HOUSE J 3 a. 2.4.

4. "A" and "D" Coys will be under the orders of O.s.C. Right
   and Left Front Line Battalion respectively.

5. All posts, dugouts, trenches &c must be left scrupulously
   clean.

6. Completion of relief will be immediately notified by
   wire to Bn. H.Q by code word "BURY", and arrival in
   Support positions by code word "WIGAN".

7. Acknowledge.

Issued at 4.30 pm   G M Dugdale
Feb. 2nd 1918.   Capt & Adjt
                                        2/8th Bn Manchester Regt.
Distribution
Copy No. 1   199th Inf Bde   Copy No. 6 O.C B Coy   Copy No. 12 H.Q
     2   2/7th Manch R   7   O.C C Coy   13/15 War Diary
     3   C.O   8   O.C D Coy
     4   2nd in Command   9   O.C H.Q Coy   16 Spare
     5   O.C A Coy   10   R.S.M
                                    11   Q.M & T.O   II a

www.ingramcontent.com/pod-product-compliance
Lightning Source LLC
Chambersburg PA
CBHW081401160426
43193CB00013B/2082